George

An Idiots guide to why you work hard at School.

Mark & Barbara
1991

S·U·P·E·R·C·A·R·S

FERRARI F40

MARK HUGHES

a Salamander book

Published by Salamander Books Limited
LONDON • NEW YORK

A SALAMANDER BOOK

Published by Salamander Books Ltd,
52 Bedford Row,
London WC1R 4LR

ISBN 0 86101 454 5

Distributed in the United Kingdom by
Hodder & Stoughton Services,
P.O.Box 6, Mill Road,
Dunton Green, Sevenoaks,
Kent TN13 2XX

Editor: Richard Collins

Designer: Paul Johnson

Line diagrams: Maltings Partnership
(© Salamander Books Ltd)

Colour profile: Maltings Partnership
(© Salamander Books Ltd)

Filmset by Flair plan Photo-typesetting Ltd

Colour reproduction by Scantrans, Singapore

Printed in Italy

Acknowledgements
Unstinting help from many people at Ferrari and Pininfarina was given during the course of this book's preparation. In particular, I am grateful to Luca Matteoni, Pietro de Franchi and Elisa Campani of the Public Relations Department at Maranello for arranging interviews, supplying information and satisfying our photographic needs. Giovanni Razelli (Managing Director), Roberto Barbiero (Project Development), Maurizio Manfredini (Experimental) and Dario Benuzzi (Test Driver) all found time to answer my questions. At Pininfarina, Daniela Cappa was always a valuable ally, and Lorenzo Ramaciotti (General Manager, Studi e Ricerche) gave fascinating insights into the design process.

Contents

INTRODUCTION

A generation ago the fastest road cars, many of them Ferraris, were spin-offs from the race circuits, but since then the technology gulf between road and track has grown steadily wider. Or at least that was the way the course of road car development looked until the arrival of the Ferrari F40 in 1987. With breathtaking bravado, Ferrari launched this street-legal racing machine as the fastest road car ever seen.

The F40 is the first car for public sale capable of exceeding 200mph. And it gets there faster than any rival: it can accelerate to 60mph in 4.5sec, to 120mph in 11.5sec. Naturally, it has handling to match its outrageous speed. Only the Porsche 959 comes close to the F40's capabilities, yet around Ferrari's tight test track at Fiorano a 959 is reckoned to be 10 seconds a lap slower.

Ferrari has accomplished this superiority over allcomers by using racing experience to pack a formidably powerful engine into a lightweight chassis carrying race-bred suspension. The F40 is truly a racing car for the road. Indeed, so much have racing requirements dictated the car's rationale that a customer, in theory, need do little more than kit himself out in helmet and overalls to take his car to the grid.

At the heart of the F40 is the most powerful engine ever put in a road car, ignoring the activities of specialist tuners. A 2.9-litre V8 carrying twin turbochargers punches out 478bhp, 20 per cent more than the GTO from which the F40 is derived. Even the rather heavier 959, a 197mph car, has to settle for 450bhp. And, says Ferrari, another 200bhp is comfortably available for

racing versions by making relatively simple modifications.

Putting its power through a five-speed gearbox, this engine sits in an advanced chassis which uses composite materials – Kevlar, carbonfibre, glassfibre, Nomex – bonded to a steel frame to save weight and increase strength. The resulting rigidity, and the handling finesse this promotes, is one of the most impressive qualities you discover when driving an F40. The stunning bodywork, the work of Pininfarina, is also made of composites. The most powerful of all supercars is also the lightest.

The F40 has arrived at a time when the supercar market is more buoyant than ever before, earning itself instant investment status thanks to great demand from Ferrari customers. It really is a very special supercar.

F40'S FOREBEAR

The GTO, Ferrari's 189mph supercar of 1984, set a new performance benchmark, one beaten only by the F40

THE BEGINNING of the development path which led to the F40 was publicly revealed by Ferrari at the Salon International de l'Automobile Genève on 28 February 1984. Here, amid a seething mass of onlookers, the dust covers on two examples of the new Ferrari GTO (chassis 0050255 on Ferrari's own stand, 0050253 on Pininfarina's) were whipped off at 5pm precisely. This was the moment when the world first saw one of the most spectacular street-legal Ferraris ever produced.

Throughout its existence, Ferrari has traded on expertise gained from motor racing in developing its road cars, although the relationship between the two sectors of Maranello's business has become progressively more distant as time has gone by. Ferrari has not been officially involved in endurance sports car racing, historically the more significant source of cross-fertilisation, since 1973; and the skyward curve of the graph of Formula One's technological development has become increasingly irrelevant, with a few exceptions, to road car engineering. Or at least this was the way it seemed until the GTO's arrival.

The GTO showed that the old adage, 'racing improves the breed', is still appropriate. Two of the most vital factors in its towering performance – the rigidity and lightness of composite materials in the body, and the engine's twin turbochargers – were drawn directly from racing experience. And with the F40, the GTO's spiritual successor, the links between road and track have been pulled still closer.

Mindful of this significance in its new limited-production supercar, Ferrari chose to give it a romantic racing title from the past. The original GTO – Gran Turismo Omologato – from the early 1960s is one of the most revered Ferraris of all time, which is why today's elite of super-rich car collectors will pay the equivalent of 500 Fiat Unos to get their hands on one. As soon as word leaked out from Maranello that a fabulous new supercar named GTO, one which was to be homologated for racing, was on the way, the anticipation of enthusiasts was aroused. If this new GTO was really going to be a revival of the old GTO's concept, it would be a truly special car. No wonder, then, that Ferrari people judged the GTO's reception in Geneva as euphoric, and matched only by the Berlinetta Boxer's arrival.

It is worth pointing out that the new car is badged simply as a GTO, although it is often referred to as the 288GTO. The numbers follow Ferrari's modern designation system, not the old cylinder capacity formula: they stand for 2.8 litres and eight cylinders.

The new GTO might never have come into existence but for the impetus provided by a new structure of motor racing regulations. A category known as Group B was among a battery of revised rallying and sports car racing rules put into place in 1982 by the Fédération Internationale du Sport Automobile (FISA). In order to be homologated into Group B, eligible cars had to be series production GTs with a minimum of two seats built in a quantity of at least 200 over a twelve-month period. The idea could have been tailor-made for Ferrari: 200 super-exclusive road cars could be built relatively easily by such a small, flexible factory, and a further twenty or so could be manufactured for racing customers.

That was the theory, but things worked out very differently in practice. Although Group B was successfully applied to rallying, the track equivalent drew so little interest from manufacturers and racing privateers that it flopped totally. Bulging order books ensured that Ferrari GTOs and Porsche 959s were nevertheless built according to the requirements, but none found their way into serious circuit competition. While Group B rally cars – like the Audi Quattro Sport, Ford RS200, Lancia Rallye 037 and Metro 6R4 – brought a dramatic era of World Championship rallying which lasted until the end of 1987 (when they were outlawed because of their immense speed), the Group B Ferraris and Porsches became instant investments cocooned in air-conditioned garages all over the world.

At first sight you might take the GTO to be a relatively simple derivative of Ferrari's best-selling 308GTB. It has a more purposeful stance and its flanks swell out even more voluptuously over wider tyres, but the shape is essentially the same. So often in the evolution of car models the original design turns out to be the best, tinkering

Below: GTO's reasonably plush cabin is a stark contrast with the F40's bare interior. Seats are leather (complete with eyelets to keep occupants cool), fascia and doors are fully trimmed, and there are carpets on the floor – this example even has a stereo radio/cassette.

and face-lifting tending to dilute the appeal of the initial shape. But this charge cannot be levelled at the GTO: the extra length in the wheelbase and the broad-shouldered look of its flared wheel-arches make it that little bit more imposing than the GTB family.

Appearances are deceptive, for there is precious little similarity with the GTB under the surface. Raising the engine cover reveals the most fundamental difference: the GTO's V8 engine, nestling beneath its turbocharging installation, is not mounted transversely as in the GTB. Instead it lies longitudinally, Formula One style, in line with a five-speed transaxle gearbox extending behind the rear axle line. This configuration allows the engine to sit so close to the centre of the car that the front half of it is tucked ahead of the back window line, only the rear four cylinders protruding into the engine bay proper.

Since that Geneva Show in 1984, the F40 has arrived to upstage the GTO. Despite their lack of visual similarity, however, the two cars are closely related. The F40 is a derivative of the GTO, boasting a striking new body and a state-of-the-art chassis.

GTO IN DETAIL
Little shared with GTB

The GTO's engine is derived from the 268C V8 which Ferrari produced in 1983 for Lancia's LC2 endurance racing coupés, and this engine in turn is related to the standard production V8 found in the GTB/GTS and Mondial ranges. The cylinder block and heads are cast in Silumin alloy, while the block's aluminium liners are toughened by a coating of Nikasil. The crankshaft runs in five

main bearings. Bore and stroke of 3.14 × 2.80in. (79.76 × 70.99mm) – the latter the standard stroke dimension of Ferrari's roadgoing V8s – give a displacement of 174cu.in. (2855cc). This size was calculated to fall just within the FISA's 4-litre Group B class: when you multiply 2855cc by 1.4 (the 'equivalency' factor used to line up turbos with naturally aspirated engines) the GTO has a racing size of 243cu.in. (3997cc).

Four valves per cylinder Quattrovalvole heads are used, with the pair of overhead camshafts on each bank driven by toothed rubber belts with tensioners. The included angle between each pair of valves is 33° 30'. Other details of this magnificent engine include a single-piece crankshaft running in five main bearings and a compression ratio of 7.6:1. Separate Weber-Marelli fuel injection-ignition systems are provided for each bank of cylinders.

Apart from the 208 Turbo (the 2-litre 'tax break' version of the GTB for the Italian market), the GTO was Ferrari's first turbocharged road car, although the Racing Department had been producing Formula One turbos since 1981. While the Grand Prix engines used German KKK turbochargers, Ferrari rather surprisingly specified a pair of Japanese IHI turbochargers for the GTO, together with German Behr intercoolers drawing cooling air through two ducts behind the rear three-quarter windows. The two exhaust runs are linked by a balance pipe over the transaxle casing feeding a central wastegate valve exhausting above 0.8bar. A bonus of rejecting the GTB's transverse engine position is that it removes the nightmare of dissipating heat from a turbocharger squeezed between engine and bulkhead.

The use of two small turbochargers was dictated by the need for progressive power delivery in a road car: throttle lag, the perennial problem of turbos, can be reduced when a pair of compressors is used. Since smaller blowers have less

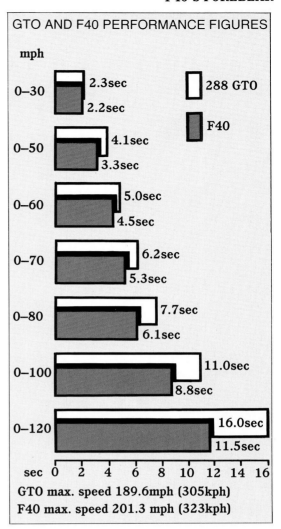

GTO AND F40 PERFORMANCE FIGURES

mph

	288 GTO	F40
0–30	2.3sec	2.2sec
0–50	4.1sec	3.3sec
0–60	5.0sec	4.5sec
0–70	6.2sec	5.3sec
0–80	7.7sec	6.1sec
0–100	11.0sec	8.8sec
0–120	16.0sec	11.5sec

sec 0 2 4 6 8 10 12 14 16

GTO max. speed 189.6mph (305kph)
F40 max. speed 201.3 mph (323kph)

Below: GTO's outline may look like a GTB's at a glance, but that array of slats on top of the engine cover hints at the 400bhp twin-turbo V8 beneath. The three slots on the rear flanks are a design signature copied from the original 250GTO sports racer of the 1960s.

Above: Comparison between GTO and F40 performance. The difference made by the F40's extra 78bhp and lighter weight is apparent all the way up the scale; F40 starts to stretch its advantage beyond 70mph; by 120mph acceleration is over 25 per cent better.

inertia, it takes less time for them to be spun by exhaust gases up to the point where they provide useful boost. The decision to use IHIs was reached after extensive testing of many turbo installations by engineers working under the direction of Nicola Materazzi. While Formula One experience showed that KKKs were ideal for producing sheer power, they presented it in a sudden rush well up the rev range. Instead IHIs were found to offer the best full-range characteristics, with the widest power spread and the most flexible response for road use. The wastegate valve is set at 0.8bar, yet even at 2500rpm the IHIs are already wound up to give 0.65bar boost.

Peak power is given as 400bhp at 7000rpm, 750rpm short of the engine's limit. Tremendous mid-range performance is ensured by the torque maximum of 366lb ft coming at a relatively low 3800rpm. In a car weighing only 2557lb (1160kg), this power produces incredible acceleration; enough to make the GTO the world's fastest road car at the time of its launch. Ferrari's own figures are 0–100kph (62.1mph) in 4.9sec and 0–200kph (124.3mph) in 15.2sec. The standing quarter-mile can be achieved in 12.7sec and the standing kilometre in 21.8sec, the terminal speed of the latter given as 156.6mph. Ferrari quoted the top speed at 305kph (189.5mph), which in 1984 was comfortably faster than any other road car, including Ferrari's own 180mph (290kph) Testarossa launched in the same year.

One benefit of the GTO's 'north–south' mechanical layout is that the engine is placed 2.8in. (71mm) lower than in the 'east–west' GTB, mak-

Below: Like a 328GTB on steroids. Overhead view of GTO shows how appearance has been beefed up by Pininfarina, with broad-shouldered wheelarches, wider wheels front and rear, 4.3in. extra length in the wheelbase and additional air outlets behind light pods.

ing the centre of gravity appreciably lower. Sitting directly behind the engine in line with the rear wheels is the beefy five-speed transaxle contained in a magnesium alloy casing. The drive is taken through an 8½in. (216mm) Borg & Beck twin-plate clutch (with hydraulic actuation borrowed from Ferrari's Formula One cars) to the gearbox, behind the final drive, and then back to the plate-type limited slip differential and through double-jointed, gaitered half-shafts. The transaxle's layout takes account of a racing customer's need for quick ratio changing by making the idler gears easily accessible through the rear cover plate. All five ratios have synchromesh, although Ferrari originally planned to offer a non-synchromesh option for racers. The forward ratios are as follows: first, 3.67:1; second, 2.28:1; third, 1.62:1; fourth, 1.27:1, fifth, 0.76:1. Reverse ratio is 3.27:1.

STRENGTH IN BUILDING
Styling by Pininfarina
The GTO's high-tensile tubular steel chassis frame is a lengthened and heavily re-worked version of the GTB's, with the wheelbase 4.3in. (109mm) longer at 96.5in (2428mm). The structure incorporates a roll-over bar and provides two tubular side frames which run either side of the engine/gearbox unit. The front track of 61.4in. (1560mm) and rear track of 61.5in. (1562mm) are both 4in. (101mm) wider than the GTB's dimensions. Overall length, too, increases by 2.4in. (61mm) to 168.9in. (4290mm).

Suspension basically follows GTB practice. There are tubular steel double wishbones at front and rear, all but the upper fronts having diagonal bracing members. An anti-roll bar is fitted at each end, while Koni adjustable co-axial coil spring and damper units are used all round. In order to

minimise the overall suspension height at the front, the spring/damper units attach to the lower part of the hub carrier and feed loads into the chassis between the upper wishbone mounting points. At the rear, where suspension height is not so critical, the spring/damper units are attached to the top of the hub carrier and protrude high into the engine bay to bear against chassis turrets which sit just below the engine cover. Steering is by rack and pinion: it is geared to give 2.9 turns from lock to lock and the turning circle is 39.4ft (12.0m).

Braking ability has to be a match for the GTO's devastating performance, so new calipers, those at the front having four-piston operation for better initial bite, were developed jointly by Ferrari and Brembo (known for their expertise with motorcycle brakes). These clasp massive ventilated discs of 12.2in. (310mm) diameter at both front and rear. A vacuum servo is included in the system. New Speedline split-rim alloy wheels with a traditional five-spoke design are used, the 8in. front rims carrying 225/50 VR 16 tyres (from Goodyear, Pirelli or Michelin) and the 10in. rears 255/50 VR 16 rubber.

Fuel consumption would not concern any GTO owner, but for the record the standard EC figures are 35.3mpg at a steady 56mph (90kph), 29.7mpg at a steady 75mph (121kph) and 15.7mpg for the urban cycle. Assuming an overall figure of 18mpg, a range of 475 miles (764km) would be possible from the twin tanks, each of 13.2 gallons (60 litres), mounted on either side of the engine bay.

As ever, the GTO's styling was entrusted to Pininfarina. A team working under Leonardo Fioravanti, Director General of Pininfarina Studi e Ricerche SpA, used a hack GTB as their starting point. After lengthening the wheelbase by the required 4.3in. (109mm), they played around with

THE ORIGINAL GTO
Incomparable beauty

What pleases the eye is a matter of taste, but the pinnacles in any field – whether architecture, painting, sculpture or even motoring – generally produce unanimity when beauty is judged. A group of car nuts may argue for hours about what they rate as the world's most beautiful machines, but a handful of automotive greats will inevitably win approval. No one would question the beauty of a Jaguar D-type, a Lamborghini Miura, a Bugatti Type 35 . . . or a Ferrari 250GTO.

The original GTO, quite simply, is one of the legends of motoring history. Many Ferraristi consider it the greatest Ferrari ever. Apart from its magnificent racing pedigree, its lines, a startling combination of grace and purpose, are quite wonderful to look at. Yet one of the surprises about the GTO is that it was shaped in-house at Ferrari, breaking with the pattern, as fixed thirty years ago as it is today, that bodies were styled by Pininfarina. Unknown engineers decided the GTO's lines, letting function dictate form. Indeed, the story goes that no drawings were made until after the first GTO had been made.

The GTO's bloodline reaches back to the 250GT of the 1950s, the family of 3-litre V12 cars which, in effect, were the first series production Ferraris. Just about the most charismatic road car available to wealthy buyers at the time, a 250GT was also a splendid tool for winning GT category motor races. Among its successes was a run of four victories, 1956–9, in the Tour de France, a 3000-mile marathon demanding speed and strength to survive over the roads, race tracks and hill-climbs which comprised this five-day event.

The derivatives which achieved this took a nickname – 250 Tour de France.

A short-wheelbase, more race-orientated version of the 250GT came in 1959 in answer to the FIA's new GT category in the World Sports Car Championship. A little stubbier but no less sleek, the 250GT SWB cleaned up just about everything in sight in the GT class, as well as taking two more Tour de France wins in 1960 and '61.

Radical rule changes were on the way during the 250GT SWB's racing career, for the FIA planned to turn the World Sports Car Championship into the preserve of GT cars, not sports prototypes, for 1962. Knowing that there was plenty of life left in the 250GT SWB, Ferrari set a team led by Giotto Bizzarrini to work on producing a whittled-down version – which would come to be called the GTO, for Gran Turismo Omologato – to take on potential rivals like the Aston Martin DB4GT Zagato and Jaguar's lightweight E-types. Close attention was paid to the aerodynamics in order partly to cure the SWB's tendency to lift at high speed, the GTO thereby earning its beautiful form.

There was nothing radical about the GTO: it was just a carefully crafted derivative of the existing hardware, using Ferrari's familiar mechanical building blocks. So it was that power came from the 250GT's 60° V12 engine, now modified to the racing Testa Rossa's specification. Displacing 180cu.in. (2953cc) from a 2.9in. (73mm) bore and 2.3in. (58.8mm) stroke, it developed 290bhp at 7400rpm: no other street-legal car could boast close to 100bhp per litre then, and even today this specific power is beyond any naturally aspirated road car. The cylinder block,

heads and crankcase were light alloy castings with pressed-in liners of cast iron. Two valves per cylinder were operated by a single chain-driven overhead camshaft on each bank of cylinders. There were six twin-barrel Weber 38DCN carburettors mounted in the vee and feeding twelve inlet ports. This magnificent power unit was mated to a new five-speed gearbox. Suspension was independent at the front, but continued to use an old-fashioned live axle at the rear.

In order to be homologated for the GT category, the rules stated that 100 cars had to be built. But only thirty-nine GTOs were made, Ferrari arguing that existing SWBs could be considered as making up the numbers since the GTO was only a 'mildly modified' version. Whether this was blatant cheating or just imaginative interpretation of the rules matters not, for the GTO was declared legal despite protests from Ferrari's competitors. It turned out to be fabulously successful in competition: it was fast and almost indestructible, a logical development of the SWB with everything put right.

Ferrari won the World Sports Car Championship three years running, in 1962–4, with the GTO and the revised GTO64. Of the twenty-eight championship events held, the GTO won twenty, finished second in fifteen and third in nine. Thereafter, Ferrari turned to rear-engined sports racers, leaving the GTO as the last of the great line of front-engined V12 racing Ferraris.

Below: The 250GTO took three consecutive World Championship titles but never won at Le Mans. It came close in 1962 – second- *place Guichet/Noblet car brushes sand at the Mulsanne Corner while third-placed 'Elde'/'Beurlys' car comes into view.*

various dummy panels until they achieved the right combination of aesthetics and aerodynamic efficiency in the Pininfarina wind tunnel. When his work was finished, Fioravanti admitted that the most challenging part of the task was to handle the change of proportion which resulted from the extra wheelbase length between the door and the rear wheelarch. His team coped well: the GTO's added length gives it an even more flowing line, which makes the GTB's classic shape look slightly dumpy by comparison.

The bulging wheelarches needed to accommodate fatter wheels and tyres (the GTO is 7.5in. (90mm) wider than the GTB) are deliciously proportioned, and the aerodynamic appendages at nose and tail are beautifully integrated into the overall shape. The tail treatment is particularly neat, the sharp flip-up on the upper surface and the row of three slots on each side behind the wheelarch conjuring up memories of the original GTO. The tail's aerodynamic lip is necessary for high speed downforce, while those three slots are a deliberate design signature, mimicking the air outlets found behind the original GTO's front wheelarches. The nose is similar to the GTB's, except for larger auxiliary lamps and a more pronounced chin spoiler, the latter again needed to generate high-speed downforce.

The air intakes scattered over the GTO's body are larger and more numerous than those puncturing the GTB's outline. The inlets at the front supply air to the water radiator, optional air-conditioning system and ventilated brakes. Three ducts on each side – along the sills, behind the side windows and in the – feed air to the intercoolers, the engine compartment and oil cooler.

A BODY OF COMPOSITES
Exploring new materials

The use of composite materials for the body was one of the most significant innovations on the GTO, especially in view of further developments which would come with the F40. The theory of composites is that different materials are incorporated into a single structure which makes the most of the individual qualities of each component, so that the panels created are both stronger and lighter than any metal equivalents. Composites played a big part in bringing the GTO's kerb weight down to 2557lb (1160kg), 227lb (102kg) lighter than the GTB; and this was achieved despite the GTO being a larger car; and, with its twin turbos, a mechanically heavier one. The other advantage of reinforced plastics is that they do not deteriorate: a GTO's body should last indefinitely.

This composites technology has been a direct spin-off from Ferrari's Formula One programme. The Racing Department began to explore composites in 1982 with the 126C2 chassis, an experimental base which led to the development of successive C3 and C4 models. One of the chief reasons for Ferrari deciding in 1981 to recruit a new English designer, Dr Harvey Postlethwaite, was his expertise with modern materials, and hence his value to them as a chassis designer. Throughout its decades in Formula One, Ferrari has always been seen as a racing car manufacturer which bolts tremendous racing engines into primitive structural hardware, its race-winning streaks coming when sheer power and driving ability overcome the chassis superiority of its predominantly English rivals. Brought in to put right this traditional shortcoming, Postlethwaite installed the facilities – including a huge autoclave, an oven for moulding composites – to work with reinforced plastics.

The activities of the Racing Department were watched closely by the production people on the other side of the road at Maranello. They realised that the GTO was their opportunity to apply this new knowledge to a road car, to experiment with expensive techniques which would have major technological implications for the future if the cost could be taken out. At this stage composites, still in their infancy at Ferrari, could be considered only for the limited-run GTO, not for series production.

A modest man, Postlethwaite has defined his role in the GTO as simply producing parts for it, not designing them. His experience in forming racing monocoques from carbonfibre, glassfibre, Kevlar, Nomex, light alloy, epoxy resin and adhesive composites helped to solve problems of rigidity, weight, noise suppression and heat isolation on the GTO. While the body was moulded essentially by using advanced glassfibre technology, some components benefited from the most pure Formula One know-how. The bulkhead between passenger compartment and engine was the most elaborate, this comprising two layers of Kevlar/glassfibre composite sandwiching an aluminium honeycomb core: this bulkhead acts as a rigid structural member; a firewall and an insulating layer. The ultra-light front bonnet lid (weighing just 7lb (3.17kg), which makes it too light to be slammed shut), roof panel and rear deck are also special pieces moulded in Kevlar/Nomex composite.

For all its visual similarity to the GTB, therefore, the GTO's composite body is one of the most important differences. The only body parts the two cars share are the steel doors and the windscreen. As well as simplifying the GTO's manufacture, keeping the existing doors made sense as their inner intrusion barriers had already passed crash test requirements in all world markets.

DRIVING THE GTO
Beaten only by F40

Opening the GTO's door reveals a cabin which could be taken for a GTB interior by any eyes but trained Ferrari-spotting ones. There are plenty of differences when you start to look around, but the first impression is of a GTB environment: there are the same doors, windscreen and instrument binnacle, the latter perched like a large orange segment on top of the fascia, which is trimmed in a black velvety material to prevent distracting reflections in the windscreen.

The seats, fairly flat in design, are very different from a GTB's leather chairs, for they are formed from Kevlar/glassfibre shells covered with black leather. Like earlier generation Ferraris, the leather is studded with rows of chromed eyelets to provide some ventilation around occupants' backsides. The interior could not be described as luxurious, nor even in keeping with the GTO's price tag, but it looks positively lavish compared with the spartan style of the F40: black carpet covers the floor and there is even space for the optional stereo radio/cassette.

Two large dials, matching the GTB's except for their higher-scale calibration in orange markings on a black background, dominate the instrument pod: a 320kph speedometer and 10,000rpm (red-lined at 7750rpm) tachometer sandwich smaller gauges for oil pressure and turbo boost. Angled towards the driver on a minimal centre console are three more small instruments for water temperature, fuel level and oil temperature. The usual three control stalks are found on the steering column, a pair on the left looking after lights and direction indicators, one on the right covering windscreen wipers and washers.

The gear lever, which sprouts through Ferrari's familiar stainless steel six-bar gate, comes straight from the later GTBs: it has the same slender, bent stem topped by a black knob. The old-fashioned finger/thumb switches, most of them controlling heating and ventilation, are like those found on early GTBs, looking as if they have been dug out from some redundant parts bin lying in a corner of the Maranello factory. You can almost imagine someone stumbling over a batch of ten-year-old switches and counting them up to see if there would be enough for 200-odd GTOs.

Below: GTO instrument panel similar to 328GTB's, but boost pressure gauge now fitted below oil pressure gauge. Speedo reads to 320kph (199mph), rev counter red-lined at 7750rpm. Unlike F40, instruments have poor clarity orange markings.

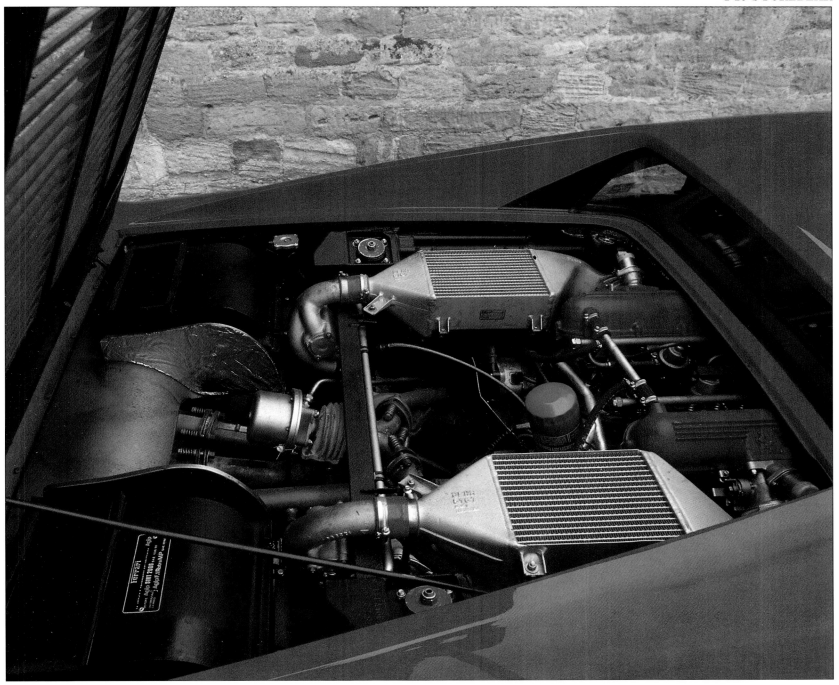

Above: Like F40, GTO engine has twin turbos and intercoolers, but capacity is smaller. While F40 engine accessibility is excellent

GTO is a mechanic's nightmare – half of engine is tucked forward of rear window line, small lid gives restricted access.

Good sized pedals, pushed off-centre by the intruding wheelarch, include a long throttle hinged from the floor, and there is a left-foot rest to help you brace your body through fast corners.

The driving position is comfortable and reasonably free of the old Italian long-arm, short-leg syndrome, although a driver over six feet might find himself short of seat travel. The small Momo steering wheel, with a chunky leather-covered rim, is pleasant to hold. Visibility, especially through the rear-view mirror, is good for such a low-slung car, but the windscreen pillars and rear buttresses create front and rear three-quarter blind spots.

The fact that this car is a cut above the GTB brings itself home as soon as you start the engine, by turning the key for ignition and pressing the rubber-clad button below to fire. The note from behind your ears is quite different from the naturally aspirated V8's metallic rasp: instead you are teased by a more mellow sound, a muffled burble characteristic of a turbo, but with enough

of a bark from the exhaust to suggest performance of a special order once the engine flexes its muscles above this civilised, even tickover. After ten minutes of restraint to let everything warm through, including the gearbox which baulks severely into second when cold, you can begin to explore the realms of exhilaration unleashed by a little more pressure on the throttle.

FLEXIBLE PERFORMANCE
Almost no turbo lag
Of course, there is quite astonishingly vivid boosted acceleration above around 3500rpm, yet the most impressive, and surprising, aspect of this twin-turbo V8 is how flexibly its performance swells up. According to the power curve, the engine develops 85 per cent of its maximum at 3500rpm, and gets better thereafter. Power comes in with a strong surge once the turbos are spinning furiously, but it is delivered with remarkable progression, flowing evenly, fulsomely, without a savage kick. Off-boost performance, with just a brush of the foot on the accelerator, is lively enough to match any common or garden supercar, but when the boost needle begins to flicker at around 2500rpm the strong push begins, turbos starting to hiss, engine note hardening, your head

lurching back if you are not braced in anticipation. The GTO picks up instantly: that wonderfully responsive engine, answering as nearly instantaneously to the throttle as any turbo can manage, catapults this red arrow forwards at a staggering rate, almost too quickly to take in.

As you give the car its 7750rpm head through the gears, figures help to clarify what dizzying speeds can be achieved in this rush of pulse-quickening, adrenalin-pumping excitement. The GTO will exceed 50mph (80kph) in first, goes on to 85mph (137kph) in second, 120mph (193kph) in third; only at 155mph (249kph) do you need to change up to fifth, which will take the car on to a 170mph canter, a 180mph (290kph) gallop and finally close to 190mph (308kph) at top whack. This lofty performance cannot be fully realised even at a tight test track like Fiorano, let alone on everyday roads. You need perfect road conditions, an empty strip of tarmac stretching far ahead, even to think about more than half-throttle, so much space does this King of Ferraris need to be exercised in anger.

For all this, the GTO is docile. It is smooth and sweet, refined and vibration-free; even the wail of the engine and wind noise are reasonably restrained. It is happy to be driven at one-tenth of its

2450

potential, which is just as well because it would otherwise be virtually unusable. Except for its gearchange and sharp clutch, it is as light and easy to control as any humble family car. Care needs to be taken to ease the clutch through its crisp biting point and the gear lever needs sharp pulls and pushes from the shoulder, but in every other respect the GTO answers to a delicate touch.

The steering is light and precise, and so effortless when you twitch the car through a turn that you would expect it to have subtle power assistance; only its weight when manoeuvring reveals that there is no power to help it. The brakes are so

capable, so solid in their response, that you never have to think consciously about using them. They act progressively to the pressure from your foot, without vibration or fade, effortlessly brushing off speed in answer to a light touch, yet stopping the car full-square in what seems a matter of yards when you squeeze harder. You need the security of massive braking power when driving a car of this potency, and this the GTO gives you.

There is enough compliancy in the suspension to give a ride quality which contributes to the GTO's relative refinement, yet the precision and tautness of the handling are worthy of a racing car with no cushioning rubber in its joints. On the

Above: First of two renderings of GTO proposals from Pininfarina shows how GTB likeness was part of the brief from the start – deep *chin spoiler and tail lip are already incorporated, but mesh grille behind rear wheel and strange red wheel rims were thankfully discarded.*

road it is rarely possible to feel any movement in the car's attitude, cornering being achieved with a totally undramatic, steer-as-you-point-it composure and a complete absence of roll. Even when pushing through a medium-speed corner with a good slice of the power tearing into the rear wheels, the tyres – larger at the back than the front, of course – keep their limpet-like grip, holding the car true to line. Through a tight

Above: Another Pininfarina study is closer to the final car, with traditional Ferrari five-spoke wheels and three air outlet slots in rear flank – *but braking cooling duct in sill has yet to appear. Those three slots are a design motif drawn from the original 250GTO.*

hairpin, like the ones which abound at Fiorano, the front end's tendency to drift wide can be neatly balanced by power oversteer, but on open roads it is difficult to provoke movement from the rear wheels in any gear. With the reserve which public roads enforce, it is impossible to force the GTO's chassis into revealing any imperfections. Even when you judge that you are driving as fast as seems safe, the car seems to leave you with vast margins of grip, its poise unruffled.

The GTO's qualities are those of any Ferrari, but they are raised to new heights in a car which provides a sublime driving experience, and one which was definitely unmatched when the GTO was new. In moving on a step further to the F40, Ferrari had only its own target to beat.

GTO'S LEGACY
A new supercar standard

The GTO seemed at the time of its launch to be a bold statement of Ferrari's technological prowess. Just as the world's great automotive styling houses produce occasionally startling prototypes to demonstrate the innovation of their thinking, so Ferrari saw in the GTO, a racing spin-off, an opportunity to show just how substantially the limits of road car performance could be re-drawn. The fact that the racing programme which prompted the GTO's development never material-

ised did not make the project any less worthwhile for Ferrari. But apart from being a new road car flagship, the GTO was a good earner too.

While the original plan for the GTO was to build the required 200 for sale to customers and a further twenty for serious competition, things worked out rather differently in practice. The twenty racers were never built, and huge demand for the roadgoing version led to a total of 278 eventually being manufactured (forty-one in 1984, 230 in 1985 and seven in 1986). All were collected from the factory by their buyers because it would have been uneconomic – and unnecessary – for Ferrari to put the car through the different homologation procedures required to sell direct in export markets.

Many customers ended up paying considerably more than the originally quoted cost, but none is complaining now about the 194,166,000 lire (around £90,000) price tag, plus – for those who specified options – 2,760,000 lire for air conditioning and 414,000 lire for electric windows. It is a mark of the GTO's exceptional qualities, even by Ferrari standards, that an example is today worth getting on for ten times its original price. And the F40 looks to be heading the same way, towards 'instant classic' status.

Indeed, the level of interest in the GTO so astounded Maranello's senior executives that the go-ahead for the F40, which cynical observers say was conceived only to tap this new vein of supercar buyers, was a mere formality. Together with Porsche and its 959, Ferrari has been responsible for opening up a booming market among the

world's wealthiest people for ultimate supercars. Today, at the start of the 1990s, plenty of rivals are jumping on the bandwagon: candidates for 200mph club membership are being developed by a staggering range of companies, from giants like Jaguar and Chevrolet to tiny manufacturers like Bugatti and Cizeta.

Never in the entire history of the motor car have more people wanted to buy machinery at the peak of the performance league, yet never before, too, have such cars been more irrelevant to daily motoring. None of the modern crop of supercars can be used to their full potential on public roads anywhere in the world, even on Germany's unrestricted but traffic-laden autobahns.

Investment is the key to this exciting aberration in the modern motor industry. The sheer romance and exhilaration of owning such an exotic supercar could never be doubted, but if you have the wherewithall to indulge in a somewhat impractical luxury it helps to know that you would see a return on your investment if you ever have to sell up. This phenomenon – who knows whether it is temporary or here to stay? – undoubtedly explains why so many people want to buy supercars right now. Once upon a time exotic sports cars depreciated just as savagely as the general run of tin boxes, but now GTOs, F40s and 959s – and, perhaps, other rivals to come – have made their mark as a sound alternative to the stock market.

This is a simple assessment of the GTO's success. It opened up a new niche in Ferrari's rarefied market, leading the company to develop a successor – the F40.

11

DESIGN AND DEVELOPMENT

How Ferrari – with a little help from Pininfarina – evolved GTO into F40, creating GTO Evoluzione along the way

WHEN THE GTO WAS launched in 1984, Ferrari had already begun work on developing its Group B racing derivative, a car which would come to be called the GTO Evoluzione. In time it became clear that the Group B racing category was to be abandoned owing to lack of manufacturer interest, but by this stage the GTO Evoluzione's transformation into a racing machine was so well advanced that it was unthinkable to consign the project to a dusty corner. Instead, it became what Giovanni Razelli, Ferrari's Managing Director, has called a 'mobile laboratory', a test bed for technology which one day might find application in road or racing cars.

Under Technical Director Nicola Materazzi, intensive work on the GTO Evoluzione proceeded, for a time without a clear idea of where this Research & Development exercise was leading. Only towards the end of the car's three-year development period was a definite purpose found for it; in July 1986, Enzo Ferrari and his Board of Directors decided to mould the laboratory GTO Evoluzione into a super-exclusive 200mph road car offering the best performance in the world. The project would become known at the factory as the LM or Le Mans, and would see light of day as the F40 – a 'marketable' version of the GTO Evoluzione.

'On 6 July last year,' said Enzo Ferrari at the F40's press launch on 21 July 1987, 'I asked my research department to look into the feasibility of building an exceptionally powerful sports car incorporating the very latest developments in engine and assembly technology. Only six days later, on 12 July, the directors gave the project their blessing, and now, barely a year later, the finished car stands before you. It is forty years since the first Ferrari left the factory. On 12 March 1947 the 125S was presented to the public for the first time. On 25 May of the same year, Franco Cortese won the Rome Grand Prix, driving a Ferrari. Now, forty years later, the Ferrari F40 demonstrates that Ferrari is still a byword for technological excellence and exceptional performance.'

Apart from making light of the development work already undertaken with the GTO Evoluzione, Ferrari did not mention how much the company had been stung into action by the arrival of the 197mph (317kph) Porsche 959, a technological tour de force which had decisively taken the mantle of the world's fastest production car to Stuttgart. There is no doubt that the real impetus behind the F40 came from the need to put the 959 in its place, and to do so with a wholly different philosophy of what the ultimate supercar should be. As Materazzi, more than any other individual the creator of the F40, says, 'I studied the 959 very closely, and found Porsche's technical solutions very interesting. But I didn't think that so much technology was right for our car. We decided to make a road car as near as possible to racing specification. It would simply be a racing car for the road, using technology necessary for the purpose, not for its own sake.'

ENGINE DEVELOPMENT
Building on the GTO

Long before the F40 had even been thought about, the first stage in developing the GTO Evoluzione was to discover how much power could be squeezed from a racing version of the GTO's 400bhp F114B engine, while keeping to the 174cu.in. (2855cc) displacement necessary to fall within the proposed 4-litre class. Retaining the existing bore and stroke measurements, Materazzi started work in late 1983 on a revised V8 engine which was given the designation F114C. It was developed in two competition forms, one state of tune (called 'Rally' and given the suffix 'R') initially developing 530bhp and a subsequent derivative (called 'Competition', but given the suffix 'K' to avoid confusion with the existing 'C' in the engine's title) starting off with a staggering 650bhp.

The F111CR achieved a 130bhp gain over the standard GTO motor with remarkably little modification. Boost pressure was increased from 0.8bar to 1.7bar, the compression ratio went up from 7.6:1 to 7.8:1, the Weber-Marelli electronic fuel injection system was modified and the valve timing was adjusted. It was enough to show the V8 engine's huge potential and to push the project on to the even more powerful F114CK stage.

Below: GTO Evoluzione's flanks show how cockpit section retains GTO and 328GTB/GTS shape, although details differ – the large NACA duct across the door is slightly broader. Note ventilation holes in rear three-quarter windows and sliding pane in side window.

When it was first run in a test cell in September 1985, the F114CK immediately delivered the 650bhp which Materazzi had expected. While most of the standard GTO engine's components remained, by now there were further modifications to the turbocharging and injection-ignition installations. Larger IHI turbochargers allowed a higher rate of airflow, but boost pressure was kept at the same formidable 1.7bar.

By late 1985, the F114CK engine was ready to be installed in the first GTO Evoluzione prototype, chassis 50253 GT, and put through thousands of test miles exclusively at Fiorano. The car would serve as a pre-F40 test vehicle for developing mechanical systems, and later as a basis for Pininfarina's work in giving it a suitably attractive body. Its appearance, with a body created by Ferrari's engineers simply to fulfil function rather than to look beautiful, was brutal and purposeful. Huge wings ballooned over wide racing tyres and the ungainly bodywork was punctured by ducts to feed air to water and oil radiators, brakes, intercoolers and the cockpit. As if to emphasise its race breeding, a two-tier wing of unpainted aluminium stuck out as a carbuncle from the rear of the car.

After Enzo Ferrari's decision that this first GTO

Below: GTO Evoluzione rear end is hardly pretty, but all the vent holes are necessary to extract hot air from engine compartment.

The finished F40 meets same requirement more elegantly, with matt black mesh across the tail panel and slots in the horizontal deck.

Evoluzione should form the basis of a new limited edition supercar aimed at road and racing use, two more GTO Evoluziones, 70167 GT and 70205 GT, were built up. The first was fitted with the 530bhp F114CR engine and the second with a variety of test engines which amounted to stages leading towards the definitive F40 unit. The margins between GTO Evoluzione and F40 are hazy, for these second and third cars can rightly be regarded also as the first F40 prototypes, since they carried Pininfarina's new body style. Rather than

Above: GTO Evoluzione tackles one of Fiorano's tight hairpins. Intensive testing at Ferrari's private track assessed the 2855cc twin-turbocharged V8 in F114CR and F114CK versions, stages in the development of the definitive 2936cc engine in the F40.

being ends in themselves, the F114CR and F114CK engines allowed Materazzi's team of engineers to study the development potential of the twin-turbocharged V8.

With the go-ahead for F40, Materazzi's task was to distill the knowledge that had been accu-

mulated into a single engine, one which would be tractable enough for road use yet at the same time offer plenty of potential for competition. The F114CR and F114CK engines both produced spectacular power high up the rev range, but a road-going unit needed also to have progressive torque characteristics at lower engine speeds.

The route chosen was to increase the capacity of the engine slightly, from 174 to 179cu.in. (2855–2936cc), by enlarging the bore from 3.14 to 3.22in. (80–82mm) and shortening the stroke from 2.8 to 2.74in. (71–69.5mm). Larger IHI turbochargers than those on the GTO were fitted and the boost pressure was set at 1.1bar (less than the GTO Evoluzione but still well above the normal GTO's 0.8bar) in order to achieve a good level of power without excessively savage delivery. A torque figure of 425lb ft at just 4000rpm matched Materazzi's objective of low-speed flexibility, while a power output of 478bhp at 7000rpm was a good increase over the GTO's 400bhp – but short of the 500bhp which Enzo Ferrari is reputed to have wanted.

Many other smaller changes were made to bring the engine to its production specification. A modified crankshaft had enlarged lubrication ducts to cope with the higher demands of racing conditions, while the pistons (designed with a pronounced 'squish' effect) were cooled by jets of oil directed into their crowns. With the help of a computer aided design programme, the camshafts were given polynomial-type cam profiles to obtain the best compromise between emissions and performance requirements. Enlarged intercoolers were mounted at an angle to improve the outflow of cooling air, and the IHI turbochargers themselves were watercooled. To cope with bottom end stresses, con rod bearings were made from a silver/cadmium alloy. The small bore increase allowed slightly larger valves, the exhaust ones having competition-derived hollow stems and heads. There was also an even more sophisticated injection-ignition system (with a multi-butterfly inlet system) than the GTO boasted.

COMPOSITES TECHNOLOGY
Exploring new materials
Inspired by the Formula One work of Harvey Postlethwaite across the road in the Racing Department, the production car side of Ferrari used

Below: Wing and slatted rear window treatment on GTO Evoluzione show further practical solutions carried over to F40.

Pininfarina's single wing for F40 in place of Evoluzione's two-tier arrangement achieves similar downforce while being more pleasing.

the GTO Evoluzione as an opportunity to build up its experience of composite materials. While the GTO's bonnet lid and engine/cockpit bulkhead had been made of composites, this limited use had only scratched the surface of the potential benefits. The new realms of road car performance being sought, it was reasoned, could be achieved just as much through the strength and weight advantages of exotic materials as by engine development.

Before wider production use of composites could be considered, however, a lengthy period of development work had to be undertaken to understand the qualities and applications of Kevlar, carbonfibre and glassfibre. Outside the Formula One world, Ferrari's only experience of building cars from non-metallic materials had come in 1975 with the first glassfibre 308GTB. This car's bodywork had worked well enough, but steel was used from 1977 to solve the problems of making an open-topped version and to counter unfavourable feedback from the all-important American market (where there was a feeling that Ferraris should not be made of 'plastic').

Composite panels are made by embedding fibrous materials with varying properties in a

mould with thermosetting resin. The thickness and alignment of these fibrous strands can be adjusted to achieve maximum strength where stresses are concentrated, such as at suspension attachments and engine mountings. An increasing range of man-made fibres is being developed, but Ferrari's F40 research focused on three types. Glass, the original type of fibre, is relatively cheap and its properties – it is basically flexible until breaking point is reached – are well understood. Kevlar is an organic fibre manufactured by Du Pont which offers great lightness but insufficient rigidity on its own. The properties of carbon fibres depend upon the manufacturing process, but those providing the best reinforcement strength are most suited to automotive use.

Although these materials are expensive, they lend themselves to short production runs because the equipment to manufacture pieces is so much cheaper than presses for producing conventional steel or aluminium panels. The designer also has flexibility because modifications to shapes and structures can be made relatively easily. The ideal manufacturing technique is to mould preimpregnated fibres in an autoclave, which controls pressure and temperature in order that the best

possible surface finish is obtained.

The most effective use of composites is to make 'sandwich' panels, where two skins enclose a core which bonds them firmly. This method exploits the best features of each material, allowing lightness and strength to be maximised. Where extra strength and ability to absorb an impact are needed, the material can be thickened with relatively little increase in weight. Sandwich structures with a core thickness of between 0.2 and 0.4in. (5–10mm) are sufficient for bodywork, while structural panels require a core 0.4–0.8in. (10–20mm) thick.

One of the special features of a composite panel is that its materials behave differently from metals according to the direction in which forces act. While this presents complex design problems in choosing materials and deciding upon their optimum alignment, it also gives immense possibilities for saving weight by arranging composite panels according to the way in which they act most efficiently.

While the theoretical advantages of composite materials – essentially they give greater strength for less weight – were understood at Ferrari, considerable experimentation was needed to discover just how they could most effectively be used. Only with the thorough knowledge gained from practical application could composites be used extensively in a road car. Ferrari's Formula One cars, which have been constructed from

carbonfibre since 1983, have provided much of this knowledge, but at the same time other avenues of research have been necessary to apply composites to mass production.

Two experimental road cars played their part in the F40's development. Both used composites for the main structure, and both were constructed as convertibles since an open body style presents more difficult problems in terms of strength. The first experimental car used Mondial mid-engined running gear attached to a central passenger compartment. Metal inserts were used to improve the distribution of stresses at the points where the engine/gearbox subframe and front suspension were attached, but otherwise the entire chassis structure was made from composites. Parts of the bodywork – bonnet, boot and bumpers among them – were also made from composites. As well as revealing the performance improvements available from a lighter structure, this experimental car also demonstrated the durability and corrosion resistance of composites.

Devised by Sergio Scaglietti, the second experimental car was a four-seater cabriolet with a well finished, but unique, appearance. Indeed, a few press photographers assumed that they were catching a scoop of a new production model, much to the delight of the engineers involved with it – they quite welcomed press attention being deflected away from the LM! The car used the front-mounted 5-litre V12 engine and rear-wheel drive transmission from the 412 2+2, and the passenger compartment was constructed to similar dimensions as the 412. This was a deliberate strategy, since it would give meaningful weight and strength comparisons between two mechanically identical cars.

This second test-bed was more significant, for it took the use of composites a stage further by using a single piece bodyshell 'compartment' fixed to a light metal frame joining the front and rear mechanical units. It raised the possibility of one day forming a composite sandwich body/chassis unit from a single autoclave pressing operation. The strength and weight advantages were spectacular: the entire car weighed several hundred kilograms less than the metal equivalent, yet torsional rigidity was improved nearly five-fold. In fact, the weight saving was so substantial that the structure was deemed almost too light for stability.

All this accumulated experience had a bearing on the final form of the F40's chassis and body,

Above: How composites perform when used structurally was evaluated in testing with this one-off cabriolet devised by Sergio Scaglietti. Its one-piece bodyshell was mated to 412 mechanicals so that direct comparisons could be made with steel-bodied car.

but there were limitations on how much composite technology could be sold to customers. The way the F40 was designed for mass production – albeit on a small scale – had to take account of the facilities available at the suppliers engaged to make composite panels on Ferrari's behalf, and on the need to be confident that the car would perform reliably over many years.

'We decided that the structural panels had to be made from carbonfibre and Kevlar because this material is fairly easy to make,' says Roberto Barbiero, who heads Project Development at Maranello. 'We wanted to use only carbonfibre, but this was not possible for production in the time available. We had to choose methods which our three suppliers could handle, because manufacture from carbonfibre alone requires more advanced facilities, such as a large autoclave, than they had available. Although the technology has been developed at Maranello, it is not possible to manufacture the pieces here. It would also not have been possible to make cars at the required production rate if only carbonfibre was used. So for F40 we felt we had to accept a level of technology which fell short of Formula One.'

While the F40's body panels are all made from carbon/glass/Kevlar composite, Ferrari decided that the chassis had to be a safe compromise between traditional and advanced technology. The objectives, therefore, were to use methods which would not create production difficulties, to save around 20 per cent in weight compared with a normal steel chassis, and to increase strength by a factor of three. The solution was to retain a lightened steel chassis braced by composite panels attached with special structural adhesive; steel was needed to form attachment points for mechanical parts.

As Formula One has shown, more radical chassis construction, without steel, is technologically possible, but not desirable for a customer car. As Barbiero says, 'A Formula One car is used for two hours in a race; the F40 is built to last for twenty years or more. Making a lighter car would have lost some of the security which the occupants must have, and would have caused homologation problems. But we can take further steps along this technological path in the future.'

GIOVANNI RAZELLI
Ferrari, Fiat, the future
At the age of forty-five, Giovanni Battista Razelli is younger than Enzo Ferrari was when the first Ferrari was manufactured. Razelli may seem youthful to be Managing Director of Ferrari, but undoubtedly he has the right pedigree after more than twenty years with Fiat. He represents today's management trend at Ferrari, for most of the company's senior personnel are Fiat hot-shots on their way up the corporate ladder. Like many of his aides, Razelli is pausing on a rung – albeit a glamorous one – during his stay at Ferrari before moving on to take charge of another colony in the Fiat empire.

Apart from a short spell with a machine tool company, Razelli has been a Fiat man since graduating from university in his home city of Genoa. He worked in Fiat design, then production and finally sales before taking up his present post upon Giovanni Sguazzini's retirement at the beginning of 1986. It was soon after his arrival, therefore, that the Ferrari F40 was conceived.

Hughes: *Work began on the F40 in the summer of 1986 and the finished car was revealed just a year later. How was such a rapid development programme possible?*

Razelli: We were able to produce the F40 so quickly because we had done so much work with our laboratory car, the GTO Evoluzione. The technical solutions of the GTO Evoluzione were very close to the F40. When we felt that the GTO Evoluzione was ready from every point of view, we decided to build up a new version for production and sale to customers. With our technical solutions achieved, our task in effect was to choose the shape to fit around them. Therefore it was possible to build up the prototype in one year.

Hughes: *The car is called the F40 because of the 40th anniversary of Ferrari: was it conceived for this anniversary, or is that a coincidence?*

Razelli: Enzo Ferrari wanted to have something special to reaffirm the company's ability to build the world's fastest road car, not to recognise an anniversary. We decided that we must always stay ahead of any rivals, such as Lamborghini or Porsche. When it came to produce the car, we found that we had an opportunity to choose a name to recognise the anniversary. The name in the factory during the F40's development was LM, for Le Mans. In Ferrari history, LM has been used for racing versions of a car, so it seemed appropriate for such a special car designed also for racing. The F40 name came later when someone suggested it.

Hughes: *There was a racing philosophy behind the car's conception, but is it likely that anyone will race an F40?*

Razelli: We are working on two versions of the F40. One is a homologated version for racing, called the F40 Le Mans, which cannot be driven on normal roads. It will be lighter and have 200bhp more. Our intention is that some customers will race in the new GTC category of the Sports-Prototype World Championship. But the racing programme will only be in the hands of customers and Ferrari importers: we have enough with Formula One.

Hughes: *F40 evolved from the GTO, which came into being as a design for the Group B racing category. Without this original Group B impetus, would this same line of evolution have been explored?*

Razelli: GTO Evoluzione was far more than a development of the GTO. It was the first test-bed for the F40, and we had our end result in mind when we embarked on this programme.

Hughes: *Was the F40 always intended to be the fastest road car in the world? Was the Porsche 959 one of the rivals you felt you had to beat?*

Razelli: Yes, of course the F40 had to be the fastest. We are Ferrari, and we are in the business of building fast sports cars. It is essential that we build the fastest car in the world. The Porsche 959 is a totally different type of car. Porsche wanted to show that they could build a technologically advanced car, but it is not a good car to race. Like Porsche, we are working on new technology: we have built laboratory cars, like the 408 for example, to test our technological thinking, but F40 was built for a different target. It is very important for the fastest car to be a Ferrari: this is our history. We must be at the top. It is not possible for us to go down.

Hughes: *Is there more to come in the future?*

Razelli: In the future I think that the competition will become stronger and more interesting. The competition is going up sharply, so we have to improve even more sharply.

Hughes: *The Porsche 959 was the fastest car for two or three years, not a Ferrari. Did its existence push you to develop the F40?*

Razelli: When the Porsche 959 came out as a car capable of 317kph, yes, we had to do something more. The only thing which matters in the competition with Porsche is maximum speed. We have no desire to match their production levels.

Hughes: *What is your answer to those people who have said that the F40, fast and brilliant though it is, is not a technologically advanced car except in its use of composite materials?*

Razelli: No one in the world today is able to build an engine to match the F40's. You can judge whether that is advanced technology or not: in my opinion it is. Four-wheel drive, as the Porsche 959 has, is not useful for this kind of car. We are not building up a car to take part in rallies, where four-wheel drive is necessary. If you go to race at Imola, Monza or Silverstone, you will find that the F40 can beat a Porsche 959 by 10 seconds per lap. If we had thought that the F40 needed other

Above: Giovanni Battista Razelli – Ferrari's Managing Director through the period of F40's design and development: 'We are Ferrari, and we are in the business of building fast sports cars. It is very important for the fastest car to be a Ferrari . . . We must be at the top. It is not possible for us to go down.'

areas of technology, we would have designed it that way. We have built a laboratory car with four-wheel drive and four-wheel steering, for example, but we will not put this type of technology in our cars until we believe there is a need for it.

Hughes: *When the F40 was introduced, we were told that 400 would be built, but now we know that there will be more. Have you decided how many?*

Razelli: We are trying not to stop! We had more than 2000 requests for the F40, so our answer to these potential customers was that the number was undecided. We have done this to try to stop the price speculation which we saw with the GTO. We know how many we shall manufacture, but we don't want to clarify the number for this reason. We don't want to build up too many because they are very special, and it is impossible with this car to manufacture more than two per day. All I can say is that the total will be less than 1000. The plan is that we shall have finished building F40s roughly by the end of 1989. There is a good reason to stop at this time because several European markets will make catalytic converters obligatory from the start of 1990. We can build F40s with catalytic converters, but customers at this level of the market want the ultimate performance and power – the requirements for this kind of car are unique. The federalised version for the USA has a catalytic converter: it makes the car a little slower, since there is 20bhp less.

Hughes: *You talk about the problems of price speculation, and we already know that GTOs have sold for ten times their original cost. Is there anything you can do to control this?*

Razelli: It could be proposed that we should minimise speculation by increasing production to meet demand, but we are convinced that Ferrari must not build too many cars. It is important to remain exclusive. But we also want to avoid the fluctuations in production – a problem when so much labour goes into each car – which would result if we produced to match demand. Our wish for the future is to remain close to our existing volumes.

Hughes: *The supercar market is surprisingly strong, more so than ever before, yet today's legal climate makes the potential of these cars impossible to realise on public roads almost anywhere in the world. Does this ever worry you for your future aim of continuing to build the world's fastest car?*

Razelli: My opinion is that we are returning to the style of the 1960s, when our customers raced their road cars at weekends. With the F40, you can go to Mugello or Silverstone at the weekend to experience sensations which ordinary cars cannot give you. The Ferrari Owners' Club in England organises a race series for this reason, and this is good. In the future, the way customers use our cars will be more specialised than today. You will go to a sports place to use a sports car, and you will use your family car to go out to dinner. The USA has the hardest speed limits yet the Americans are our best customers: they believe in different uses for different cars. I don't think the law-makers are a problem for our market.

PININFARINA'S ROLE
A new suit of clothes

When Ferrari decided to market its street version of the GTO Evoluzione something undoubtedly had to be done about its crude appearance. Ferraris must be beautiful: the GTO Evoluzione, its shape formed by functional need, was downright ugly.

Pininfarina, the Turin-based car design house which has enjoyed a virtual monopoly in winning Ferrari styling contracts these thirty years past, was called in to handle the brief. In July 1986, just a few weeks after Ferrari's go-ahead for the so-called LM, a small team of designers began sketching ideas at Pininfarina Studi e Ricerche SpA, working under General Manager Leonardo Fioravanti and Deputy General Manager Lorenzo Ramaciotti. Time was short, and the parameters within which they had to work were tight.

'Ferrari asked us to give the GTO Evoluzione a more appealing appearance without spoiling the aerodynamic behaviour which had been achieved,' says Ramaciotti. 'We also had to take into account the cooling needs of the mechanical parts which had already been satisfied on the GTO Evoluzione.

So our brief was to design a new front and rear for the car, but to leave the central passenger cell unaltered. Our design had to achieve the same drag and downforce values as the GTO Evoluzione, and it was necessary to keep the dimensions and positions of all air intakes while giving them a more sophisticated and less functional look.'

The schedule imposed great pressure. Ferrari wanted the car to be launched within a year, so Pininfarina's design procedures had to be telescoped into a third of the normal gestation time. It seemed a tall order, but not an impossible one; after all, the mechanical layout of the car was established. In effect, Pininfarina was being asked merely to cast back to an earlier era, when it was commonplace to develop conceptually similar road-legal sports racers, such as the GTO or SWB, in a remarkably short time.

'Ferraris used to be created in less than a year,' said Fioravanti in his speech at the F40's press launch: 'The result of our so-called progress – the evolution and changing of the times, in any case – is that even today's Ferraris take three to four years to conceive, design and build, sometimes

Above: Two shots taken in Pininfarina's presentation hall of the polyurethane foam model used for wind tunnel testing. The shape is almost identical to a real F40's, but differences include paired exhaust outlets behind the rear wheels (instead of three pipes in the centre) and a stepped bonnet lip.

longer. In this instance, the entire Ferrari and Pininfarina team confronted the problem without what I would call the 'manias' of today: we approached the design of this car like we used to, forcibly inserting it into other programmes, working at impossible hours.'

Where dramatic short cuts could be made, Pininfarina decided, was in the early stages of sketching. The usual practice is to refine a design through a series of renderings, gain Ferrari's approval for the basic shape, make full-scale section drawings and then build the first full-scale model. For the F40, however, a year's worth of work was completed in a matter of weeks.

'Only a couple of months were available to produce a model for wind tunnel testing,' says Ramaciotti, 'so we didn't make as detailed a mock-up as we usually would. Before any section drawings were made, we produced a single polyurethane foam model which was used for developing the shape and then testing the aerodynamics. We started by making some sketches to visualise ideas and details, but they were not very close to the finished car. There are some details which you can recognise, but that's all. Instead of choosing one design, we used these renderings as reference themes which crystallised as we worked directly on the foam. The car was designed in three dimensions in the shop. Normally we would make a full-scale section drawing to develop a model, but in F40's case the model came before any drawings.'

Pininfarina kindly released some of these thematic renderings for publication in this book, and they confirm how little the F40's shape had been determined by the time the foam model was made. Piero Camardella's interpretation is clearly no more than a refined version of the GTO Evoluzione: the nose and tail of this proposal are busy (with an odd double wing arrangement at the rear), but the rounded form of the body is little altered in general. Aldo Brovarone's sketch contains stronger hints of F40, particularly in the integrated rear wing, the angularity of the body and the profile of the rear window; but even so the design has a long way to mature.

By refining the foam model – cutting away here, building up the profile there – a fairly accurate outline of the finished F40 was created. Lack of time meant that it was given only a coat of matt paint when presented to Ferrari, but how the shape would perform in the Pininfarina wind tunnel was what mattered. While wind tunnel testing would bring detailed changes to meet all the aerodynamic needs, the basic design philosophy was established: the F40 was intended to convey traditional Ferrari design themes within a strikingly purposeful shape.

'We derived some of our ideas from racing Ferraris of the past,' says Ramaciotti. 'For instance, the theme of the three air intakes at the front is very typical of Ferrari racing tradition – a large central intake for the radiator and two small intakes on each side for the brakes. Above these intakes, lights are enclosed behind two transparent fairings. This was the pattern of the front of Ferrari racing cars of the 1960s; we have tried to recreate this on the F40 while fulfilling the functional needs established with the GTO Evoluzione. There is a very strict relationship in form and function between old and new.

'The same thinking was applied to the rear of the F40. We made a full-width spoiler for aerodynamic purposes, instead of the GTO Evoluzione's design which was more reminiscent of a racing car. That type of wing was not possible for road use because the edges are too sharp, and the way in which it blended with the fins either side of the rear window was less efficient aerodynamically. We looked for something more integrated; the style we chose was like the 312P, the Ferrari sports prototype racer of the early 1970s.

'Some inspiration also came from modern Group C racing cars, as you might expect in view of the fact that F40s will be raced. Sports racing cars are not rounded: they have square shapes on soft curves. A Jaguar Group C car, for example, has flat sides but quite a round cockpit. So we put roundness into the F40's shape where it was necessary, as in the rear window area. But there are relatively flat areas: the sides must be quite square because the body must wrap closely around the wheels. The car has the amount of roundness needed for the purpose.'

Wind tunnel evaluation with the foam model

began just two months after the first sketches had been drawn. This was an important stage, for aerodynamic excellence is a vital part of the make-up of a 200mph road car. Working on a combination of experience and hunch, Pininfarina's team knew that they had the F40 about right at the foam model stage, but plenty of aerodynamic fine tuning is always needed before all the requirements are met. As well as being slippery

enough to exceed 200mph with the available power, the F40 also had to offer the front and rear downforce values necessary for it to be stable at all speeds.

A wind tunnel is a very sophisticated tool, but it cannot provide the designers with answers to their problems. The speed with which this stage of the design process can be accomplished depends on how well the stylists have done their job in the

Above and below:
Pininfarina stylists expressed their initial F40 design thoughts in the usual way by preparing renderings

– but these were used only for crystallising ideas prior to forming the shape directly on the foam model. Piero Camardella's three sketches

(above) show little more than a refined version of GTO Evoluzione. Aldo Brovarone's ideas (below) contain more hints of the

finished F40 in rear wing treatment, teardrop shape of back window, two channels in rear under-valance and flattened nose surface.

Above and below: Part of Pininfarina's photographic record of the F40 foam mock-up during stages of wind tunnel testing – visible in each shot is the test number. Test 4 has plenty of bare foam exposed and the rear wing missing. Test 5 has a more discreet version of the windscreen wiper fairing, which was visible so prominently on the unsullied foam model. Test 10 shows a different front spoiler section with squarer edges to the water radiator and front brake ducts, although these still differ from the finished shape. Test 12 has the wing uprights in place but not the wing itself. Test 15 shows that, despite modern techniques of using pressure sensors and electronic scans of pressure patterns, Pininfarina still feels that the old-fashioned wool tuft method has a place in wind tunnel experiments, quite simply, the tufts are blown straight where air flows smoothly over flat areas of the body, but eddies are created around air intakes and outlets.

SUPERCARS: FERRARI F40

first place. Each experiment in the wind tunnel gives a range of information which must then be interpreted to find better solutions. It tells the technicians if any modification is an improvement or not, but it does not tell them what the modifications should be. Gradually, as test after test is carried out, tiny changes are made to wing profiles, air intake patterns and body panel shapes in order to reach the end result. Typically, the long process of the F40's wind tunnel evolution was a case of myriad small improvements adding up to produce the ideal whole.

Computer scans of the slipstream behind the car helped to refine the shape of the rear. Considerable energy can be lost if there is turbulence where the airflow detaches itself from the car, so a clean 'wake' is essential. Using recently developed methods, Pininfarina was able to make electronic scans to measure sections of pressures at various distances from the tail, this information being processed by a computer to produce a coloured image of airflow patterns on a video screen. This gave an instant picture of the shape of the slipstream, so that the effect of different body forms at the tail could be observed. All these modern wind tunnel procedures – a far cry from the old-fashioned approach of studying the movement of hundreds of wool tufts applied to the car's surface – give a very clear picture of aerodynamic behaviour.

'Straight away it was clear that we were starting off with a good shape,' says Ramaciotti, 'but that can make it all the more difficult to determine the necessary modifications. Apart from the time it all took, I would say that the wind tunnel stage went well. Our biggest problem was to improve stability by increasing the downforce at the front, which meant changing the height of the dam and the profile of the chin.

'The F40 has major aerodynamic needs because drag is very important to achieve the speed. To exceed 200mph we had to have a certain Cd, not more, but at the same time good downforce values were needed as a matter of safety for the driver. The problem was to reduce drag while at the same time increasing downforce. With an aerodynamic device it is generally very easy to increase downforce, but the trick is to do it without too much penalty in increased drag. With such a big wing at the rear, we found that it was easy to create the required downforce at that end, but it worked so well that we found it tending to reduce the downforce at the front. The problem of balancing the car to find a good front/rear downforce compromise was the focus of our work in the wind tunnel.'

The need to speed up the F40 design process did present problems. In the time available, it was impossible to create a sufficiently sophisticated foam model incorporating all the correct air intakes and outlets, so tests had to be carried out in comparison with the GTO Evoluzione dummied up to represent a 'control' condition. It had all its intakes and outlets closed off and the underbody faired in so that comparative values could be obtained. Since airflow into intakes could not be measured, pressure values at the intake positions had to suffice.

'We were not 100 per cent sure of the results until a finished F40 prototype could be tested,' says Ramaciotti, 'but in the end there was no significant difference between test conclusions and the real car. The wind tunnel is sophisticated enough for us to predict behaviour on the road. Of course there are differences in road conditions, such as the rotation of the wheels and the

Above: More pictures from the Pininfarina wind tunnel. The top photograph shows a substantially revised back end with faired-in wheels, a spoiler at the base of the tail (to give clean detachment of air from under the car) and broader wing uprights to support a longer aerofoil profile. The centre photograph shows the points where pressure sensors were attached to the three blanked-off side ducts, while the bottom photograph has the nose intakes taped over and door mirrors fitted.

bonnet. In the end it was thought to look a little strange.

Another option tried was the use of spats enclosing the rear wheels, in the style of some Group C racing machines. These fairings gave a small aerodynamic improvement which would have shown itself in a marginally higher top speed, but the advantage was not radical enough to make up for the problems of practicality. Apart from making a wheel change more difficult, wheel fairings inhibit the flow of cool air to the rear brakes and present structural difficulties in bracing the panels to keep them rigid.

Although part of Pininfarina's brief had been to retain the central passenger cell from the GTO Evoluzione (which itself was identical in this area to the GTO), some minor changes were necessary to tidy up airflow. While the roof and windscreen remained unaltered, the doors were given a slightly flatter profile and the ducts below the side windows widened.

Below: Unlike all other mid-engined production Ferraris, the F40 has a rounded rear window – made of plexiglass containing slots for engine cooling – to allow air to flow smoothly to the wing; the usual style of an upright rear window and flat engine cover creates more turbulence.

For all their sympathy with Ferrari design tradition, the Pininfarina team did make one significant departure from standard themes. Every mid-engined Ferrari road car – from 246 Dino and 308GTB to Testarossa and GTO – has featured side buttresses running backwards from each side of a small, upright rear window. This traditional feature, with the rear window in line with the engine/cockpit bulkhead, helps to isolate engine noise from the passengers and to dissipate engine heat. For an out and out road racer such as the F40, however, aerodynamic purity was deemed more important than noise suppression.

'We worked a lot on the shape of the back window,' says Ramaciotti. 'The usual style is not so effective aerodynamically because the sharp step down from the roof line creates turbulence, reducing the efficiency of the wing. By giving the window a more rounded, smoother shape – and putting slots in the plexiglass to remove heat from the engine – we allowed the rear wing to work in clean air, so improving the high speed behaviour of the car.'

Almost every detail of the F40's shape is designed for function. Even the three cowls underneath the tail are shaped to tidy up airflow from

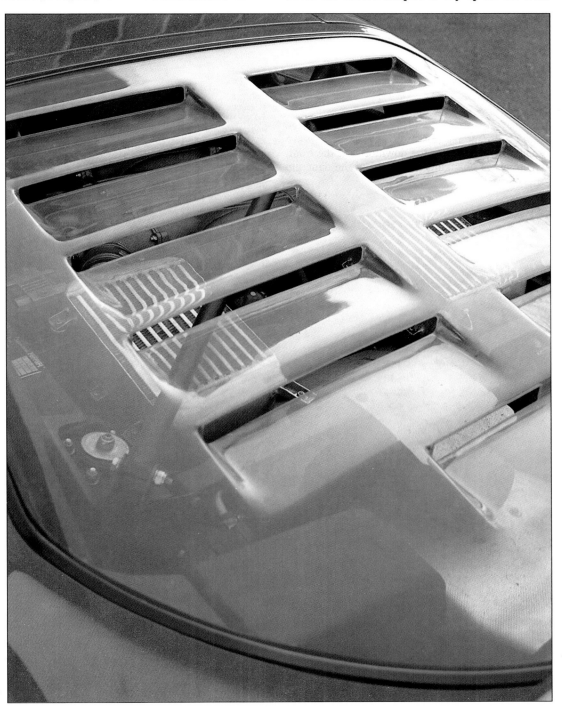

existence of different boundary layer characteristics because of the changed relationship between ground and car. But we know the correlations required to calculate these from the test data.'

Some of the differences which evolved can be spotted by studying the accompanying sequence of pictures, part of Pininfarina's photographic record of the wind tunnel process. The initial nose treatment, with a squarer profile to the central intake and a less pronounced chin below it, had to be changed, although the general sweep of the bonnet remained unaltered. Different approaches to the design at the rear were also tried, one photograph in particular showing a deeper wing and a strong lip across the base of the tail.

One change, for an aesthetic rather than functional reason, was to dispense with the asymmetrical fairing concealing the single windscreen wiper in the parked position (clearly visible in photographs of the unsullied foam model): this arrangement would also have allowed the driver a slightly better view over the lower side of the

Below: Interior of an F40 prototype looks just like a finished car at first glance, but there are small differences: relay/fuse panel around gearshift untrimmed.

in front of passenger seat is exposed, dial positions in instrument binnacle are different and central tunnel

Above: Ferrari studio shot shows that pre-production F40 prototype has the finalised body form. Notice how the black strip also seen on the Peugeot 405 and Alfa Romeo 164.

under the car, channelling the stream away from the wheels and the gearbox. The rising profile of this underbody section is reminiscent of ground effect thinking, and indeed a small contribution is made to the rear downforce value. As the rear view of the foam model shows, the outer cowls were intended to house dual exhaust pipes on each side, but space was found for a neater exhaust run through the central cowl. Virtually the only non-functional design touch is a groove (inlaid with a black strip) running all the way round the car; the purpose of this is simply to give the shape a slightly more homogenous feel.

The knowledge that composite materials would be used extensively in the F40's body and chassis influenced only the interior design. With Ferrari's blessing, Pininfarina deliberately made a feature of this technology by leaving the cockpit bare and purposeful, with large areas of composite panel-work visible. As Ramaciotti says, 'Covering the composites with padding and carpet would have added weight and detracted from the techno-logical statement of the car.'

The Pininfarina team also had to be mindful of the constraints imposed by homologation require-ments: in other words, conforming to the battery of regulations laid down by national governments in all major car-buying markets. Some of the requirements which the stylist must consider are the number and position of lighting fixtures, height of lights, ground clearance and visibility to front and rear. Since Ferrari's plan at first was to sell F40s directly from the factory, homologation was necessary only for Italy: non-Italian custom-ers would have had to make their own transport arrangements. As it turned out, it was possible to extend the F40's homologation to other countries, including the USA (where a catalytic converter must be fitted to meet exhaust emissions require-ments).

Designing door mirrors was Pininfarina's major homologation hurdle, since a compromise had to be found which met regulations governing rear-ward visibility without sacrificing hard-won

aerodynamic solutions. Mirrors were fitted only for the final stages of wind tunnel testing, when it was found that the airflow behaviour into the intakes on the car's flanks was spoiled. While road testing was in progress, a new design of mirror was

perfected. Pre-production prototypes, therefore, have the original large mirrors mounted to the quarterlight windows, while later customer F40s have slightly more discreet pod-type mirrors attached directly to the doors.

Apart from such minor details, Pininfarina's final form for the F40 was finished by the spring of 1987, ready for the tooling procedures necessary to make running prototypes and customer cars. The team of fifteen or so stylists, modellers and technicians which had worked under Fioravanti and Ramaciotti could breath a sigh of relief before turning to more mundane automotive tasks – perhaps another new Peugeot or Alfa Romeo. In retrospect, how does Ramaciotti look back on the F40 design process in comparison with other Ferrari projects?

'We knew from the start that we had to work quickly: in fact we didn't even have any warning that the project was coming. We might have worked fewer weekends and devoted more resources to it had we known in advance, but I don't think we lost anything. Sometimes the most successful projects are those you undertake with no preparation. Of course, we didn't ask ourselves whether we could do it; a project like this doesn't come up every day.

'There were remarkably few problems because the car went well from the beginning – we always knew that we were on the right track. Actually the fact that we were providing a new body for an existing car did not make the task easier. How to

reach the drag and downforce targets *and* make the car look nice was the most difficult part. There was not even much need for discussion with Ferrari; we were on the same wavelength. From the beginning there seemed to be a perfect understanding between the way we were developing the car and Ferrari's expectations.

'Other cars may be designed with more time, but you are not always certain that you are working towards the right solution. When you are not so sure of what you are doing, the pressure is greater – you have to ask yourself every day whether what you are doing is right.'

For Fioravanti, the project was refreshing and inspiring, as he explained at the conclusion of his speech at the F40's press launch: 'This car had wonderful significance for us. In this world made perhaps of too many computers, too much equipment and too many problems of all sorts, we regained the feeling of designing and building a car, if I can use the expression, with sentiment; transport, without implications of time and reasoning that I would sometimes describe as abstruse. We made a car like they used to be made.'

THE FINAL TEST PHASE
Preparing for production
Since Pininfarina's faithful foam model was not a suitable basis from which to begin tooling, its shape was translated into aluminium at the body shop of Dino Cognolato, near Padua. As well as providing a 'master' from which moulds could be made, this one-off, hand-made F40 aluminium body was a final opportunity to check any delicate highlights of the shape that had not been obvious on the matt-painted foam model.

Above: Pictures show that first F40 prototype began test work without mirrors (left), later prototypes had quarterlight-mounted mirrors which spoiled airflow behaviour into the large ducts along the doors (centre), and customer cars have pod-type mirrors attached lower down, on the doors themselves (right).

There were seven F40 prototypes. The first two were actually the second and third GTO Evoluziones, 70167 GT and 70205 GT, with F40 bodies; these cars were used largely for high-speed circuit evaluation. The third car was built up solely for motor shows and exhibitions. Three more F40 prototypes were used for road testing, one being dedicated to suspension work and another ending its homologation programme (which included braking, pollution and noise requirements) against a concrete block in the impact test. The final prototype was used as a pre-production dummy to familiarise workers with new assembly techniques.

The final F40 test phase was managed by Maurizio Manfredini of the Experimental Department. His team of drivers was headed by Dario Benuzzi (also a Formula One test driver), with Claudio Ori and Giuseppe Cornia conducting most of the work alongside Benuzzi.

'Our work with the GTO Evoluzione had been carried out only at Fiorano,' says Manfredini, 'so there was plenty to find out about road and high-speed use with the first F40, given to us in February 1987. As well as more time at Fiorano, we did a lot of work at the high-speed bowl at Nardo on maximum speed behaviour, and established the top speed as 325kph (201.9mph). With the second prototype we also went to Imola and Alfa Romeo's Balocco test track.'

Benuzzi invariably took care of the Nardo sessions, driving the F40 on public roads for the 1000km trip (over 600 miles) from Maranello to the heel of Italy. He reckons that the journey was possible in around five and a quarter hours (including fuel stops), which works out at a running average of nearly 120mph (193kph).

'The car was very pleasant and easy to drive over such a long trip,' says Benuzzi. 'Around Nardo, it is also comfortable to drive at its maximum. It is very stable, and the downforce is so good that it feels strongly attached to the road. Although its maximum speed is a lot higher than a Testarossa, I find that it is much easier to handle. It's noisier, for sure, but that is unavoidable in a car of this type; most of the noise is from the air, not the mechanicals.'

Fiorano lap times are a measure of the F40's ability. The best time achieved on road tyres during this test period was 1min 29sec, 7sec better than the GTO; on racing tyres an F40 has managed 1min 25sec. The F40's great rival, the Porsche 959, is reckoned by Benuzzi to be around 10sec a lap slower than the F40, the difference showing in straight-line speed as well as cornering ability; at the end of Fiorano's short straight

Below: Wheels have Ferrari's traditional five-spoke alloy style (which goes back more than twenty years to the Daytona), but this

Speedline design is a racing-type split-rim with a single octagonal nut secured by a pin – note drilled discs and Brembo caliper.

an F40 reaches nearly 160mph (257kph), a 959 only around 140mph (225kph).

There is a very great difference between 959 and F40,' says Benuzzi. 'The handling of the 959 is not very well suited to the track; it understeers on slow corners and oversteers on fast ones. The F40 is far more neutral to drive, and it is helped by more progressive power delivery. I don't find the 959's balance right for the track, but it is a fine car for the road. The F40, however, is good on the road and the track.'

Gerhard Berger, one of Ferrari's Formula One drivers at the time of writing (and an F40 owner), also put in some test miles with F40 prototypes, and his opinions about the car were quoted in *Autocar* magazine (8 June 1988): 'I have driven a lot of F40 prototypes, and the early engines were much more malicious than the production specification. The engine is now tuned for everyday use and runs fantastically well. It bites from around 3000rpm and upwards of 3500rpm it really takes off, as if the turbos are constantly supplying full boost. I like hard-tuned suspensions, and the F40 has the best road chassis I have ever driven. If you are experienced with racing cars, the F40 is very easy to drive.'

Below: F40 in the Apennine foothills, where quiet, twisty roads provide an ideal test route just a few miles from the factory. Plenty of

evaluation was done at Fiorano and Nardo, but road mileage was necessary to find how the car behaves in a range of conditions.

With so much work on the F40's mechanical make-up having been achieved during the GTO Evoluzione programme, relatively few modifications had to be made through this final test phase. Manfredini points to three specific areas: 'First, the brakes take a lot of punishment on such a fast car, so quite a lot of work had to be done to lower brake temperatures and remove vibration. We also started with servo-assistance, but when this was removed we found that we gained more feel through the pedal without adding too much to the pressure. Second, high-speed testing showed that minor aerodynamic modifications were needed to the front of the spoiler and the rear of the undertray, but generally Pininfarina did an incredible job with the body – it worked well from the start. Third, a lot of effort also had to go into finding the best tyres to put the power to the road; by the time we had finished testing many types of tyres, we had increased the size of the rear rims from 10 to 13in.

Testing was carried out before and after the F40's press launch in Maranello on 21 July 1987. Once the customer production specification had been fixed by early 1988, three months before production began, Manfredini and his team got their teeth into the F40 Evoluzione racing derivative; but for delays in this programme, the car would have raced during 1989.

A few words are needed about the choice of name. During its early stages of development, as

we have seen, the car became known to everyone at Maranello as the Le Mans since there were clear spiritual links between this new 'berlinetta' and the very first rear-engined customer road/race car, derived from the 250P which won Le Mans in 1963. The company has always stated that the car was conceived to celebrate Enzo Ferrari's forty years as a car manufacturer, but the title F40 was settled on only shortly before launch. No one will say, but it could be that the anniversary turned out to be a convenient coincidence, not part of the rationale for creating the car. In his book, *Enzo Ferrari. The Man*, Gino Rancati relates how he was first shown the car on 4 June 1987 by Giovanni Razelli, who asked him for ideas for a name. Rancati suggested 'Ferrari Forty' ('Quaranta' in Italian), and later received a silver plaque from Razelli with the inscription, 'To Gino Rancati for a brilliant idea'.

The final verdict on the F40's birth should belong to Nicola Materazzi, the key man in the whole programme: 'This car is my son. It was very exciting to work on, and even more exciting to drive. Its performance always astonishes me. Quite simply it is the nearest thing to a racing car that you can take out on the road.'

Right: Would you like one parked outside your front door? At the time of writing, Ferrari had yet to reveal exactly how many F40s

would be made in an attempt to keep the price speculators in the dark – Giovanni Razelli's only word is that the total will be fewer than 1000.

INDUSTRIE PININFARINA SPA
Stylists with vision

So many coachbuilders, most of them Italian, have been responsible for Ferrari styling in the past that the list reads like a roll-call of the greatest ever car designers: Allemano, Bertone, Boano, Fantuzzi, Stabilimenti, Farina, Frua, Ghia, Neri and Bonacini, Scaglietti, Touring, Vignale, Zagato . . . to name but a few. But one company towers above all these – Pininfarina.

Most of these famous names have faded away, casualties of changing times, of the move away from hand-crafted coachbuilding towards mass-production at the exotic end of the market. Pininfarina, on the other hand, has grown into a substantial manufacturing and design consultancy empire with a brigade of heavyweight clients, none of them more valued than Ferrari.

PININFARINA AND FERRARI
A remarkable relationship since 1952

For more than a generation Pininfarina has enjoyed a remarkably intimate relationship with the world's most glamorous car maker. You might expect their association to be a precarious one, since a car styling studio is only as good as its last design; one falter on Pininfarina's part and Ferrari could turn elsewhere the next time. Yet only once in more than twenty years has Ferrari approached another designer to sketch a new production car, and that was Nuccio Bertone for the 308GT4 of 1973; Giorgetto Giugiaro and Marcello Gandini, two of the

very best, have not had a look in.

The amazing thing about Pininfarina is that it always produces sensational looking cars for Ferrari. The company founded by Battista 'Pinin' Farina has a brilliant record in creating beautiful, timeless shapes to clothe Ferrari's charismatic engineering. Throughout automotive history only Bugatti has combined elegant engineering and aesthetic quality as successfully as the Ferrari/Pininfarina liaison.

While the F40 is the latest fruit of this unique collaboration, Pininfarina and Ferrari go back to 1952, when a two-seater cabriolet body was designed for the 212 Inter. Its low-slung lines and smooth flanks were very pure by the standards of the day, but Pininfarina also impressed its client with how successfully it solved the torsional rigidity problems of building an open car on a tubular frame. Only the car's heavily chromed egg-crate grille jars the eye today.

Over the years Pininfarina has generally followed an evolutionary path in its work for Ferrari, developing existing styling themes a little further with each new model. The 212 Inter was followed by the 342 America, with its front grille thrust forwards between the headlights, and then on the 375 America the grille took on a squarer appearance. Yet at the same time it has occasionally produced a radical departure, such as the 375MM berlinetta displayed at the 1954 Paris Salon. Built for Ingrid Bergman, this stunning machine was a perfect showcase for aerodynamic ideas: the headlights were retractable, the bonnet line plunged down to a very low

grille and buttress panels extended backwards from each side of the rear window in a style later resurrected for Dino, 308GTB and Testarossa.

Great Pininfarina Ferraris tumbled out of Turin so quickly over the next few years that it is difficult to isolate the most handsome: all manner of coupé 250GT bodies, culminating in the supreme Berlinetta Lusso of 1962; delicious 250GT convertibles, like the 1958 Spyder California; and imposing 410 and 400 Superamericas. Many styles were produced in small numbers, each with tiny differences which can be spotted only by a trained eye; and for favoured customers, like Prince Bernhard of Holland, Pininfarina could always create a one-off design.

The proliferation of special coachwork declined as the 1960s progressed and Ferrari production turned more towards standard models, but Pininfarina's work was no less arresting. The brutally elegant 275GTB, the timeless Daytona and the trend setting Dino (the first mid-engined Ferrari road car) stand out as the great shapes of this decade.

The three classics of the 1970s were the 308GTB, the 365GT4 2+2 and the Berlinetta Boxer, all of them quite different in conception. The mid-engined 308GTB took the Dino philosophy a stage further with another enduring, curvacious shape which looks as fresh today as when it appeared fifteen years ago. The charismatic Boxer is altogether more muscular, but beautifully proportioned nonetheless. As for the 365GT4 2+2, the fact that its regal, crisp shape is still in production – as the 412 – eighteen years after launch shows how well it has worn. It speaks volumes for Pininfarina's reputation that Bertone's 308GT4 is the only Ferrari of the past twenty-five years whose looks have not been universally appreciated – and largely because of this it remains the cheapest Ferrari in today's classic car bull-market.

PININFARINA BEYOND FERRARI
Designing for other car makers

Ferraris, however, have been only the icing on Pininfarina's cake, for many other motor manufacturers have been clients. Peugeot has a historic association with the design house which began with the 403 of 1955, continued with the 504 of 1968 in gawky saloon and pleasing cabriolet versions, and comes right up to date with the French manufacturer's best selling 205 and 405 model ranges, which are surely two of the best looking ordinary cars currently on the market. Many of the products of Italy's car giants – Fiat, Lancia and Alfa Romeo – have also begun life at Pininfarina. Great Lancias include the 1951 Aurelia B20, the 1955 Aurelia Spyder, the 1975 Beta Monte Carlo and the 1976 Gamma Coupé. Among the Fiats have been the gorgeous razor-edged 130 Coupé of 1971 and the 124 Spider sports car launched in 1967, this latter built by Pininfarina and in its closing years actually badged as the Pininfarina Spidereuropa – more than

Left: Sergio Pininfarina and Ferrari Testarossa at Pininfarina's Cambiano Studi e Ricerche facility, where new designs are *conceived. The son of the founder, Sergio has been in control since 1966, but is now handing over the reins to the third generation.*

200,000 were produced up to 1985. Alfa Romeo's association stretches back to the 1955 Giulietta Spyder and exists today in the form of the 164, the new executive saloon which looks set to revive this sporting marque's fortunes after years of decline.

British manufacturers have also turned to Turin for inspiration. Two BMC stalwarts, the 1958 Austin A40 and 1962 Morris/Austin 1100, were designed by Pininfarina, as well as an outstanding 1967 aerodynamic concept car which BMC regrettably turned down – and which undoubtedly inspired the Citroën CX. The only occasion when Rolls-Royce has commissioned an outside designer occurred in 1975 when the Camargue was launched; this two-door coupé is not one of Pininfarina's best efforts, but the company is proud of its association with Rolls-Royce. A wonderful redesign of the Jaguar XJ-S in 1978 was never more than an independent styling exercise, but its fluid evolution of the E-type's shape put the XJ-S's uncomfortable styling well and truly in the shade.

THE FAMILY FIRM
More than a design house

Pininfarina has always been more than a design house. After breaking away from his brother's company, Stabilimenti Farina, Battista 'Pinin' Farina established Carrozzeria Pinin Farina in 1930. His intention was to expand the craft of building special car bodies into a small-scale industry, by designing and manufacturing complete cars on behalf of other car makers – his early success can be

Below: Battista 'Pinin' Farina (left) and Enzo Ferrari began their historical association with a 212 Inter convertible design in 1952. Pininfarina has styled more Ferraris than any other coachbuilder.

measured by the fact that he employed 500 people by the outbreak of World War II. Exactly the same function is performed today, except that the enterprise, with a workforce of over 2000, is rather larger.

While the creative people work in secrecy at the Studi e Ricerche facility in Cambiano, a small town twenty miles east of Turin, the manufacturing plant of Grugliasco, a Turin suburb, makes complete Pininfarina-conceived cars. Currently the output of around 30,000 cars a year comprises Cadillac Allantés (shipped to the USA aboard specially converted Jumbos), Lancia Thema estate cars, Peugeot 205GTI cabriolets and Alfa Romeo Spiders, as well as fully-trimmed and painted bodyshells for Ferrari Testarossas and 412s.

Battista 'Pinin' Farina (his nickname, meaning 'small', stuck so firmly that he merged the two words in 1961) died in 1966, but the company remains true to his vision and still under family management. Sergio has been in control since his father's death, but nowadays his time commitments as head of the Italian equivalent of the CBI have meant that the third generation of Pininfarinas is coming to the fore: Paolo is in charge of liaison between design and production, while Andrea manages the manufacturing side of the business. Continuity with the past is important for the future.

And that future looks set to include many more Ferraris. The F40 is just the latest chapter of a book which is still being written.

F40 IN DETAIL

Extraordinary power, race-bred suspension and an innovative chassis — a close look at the world's fastest road car

To HOLD THE MANTLE of the world's fastest car means that the F40 is inevitably technologically very special, yet at the same time it is a very simple car. Its advanced technology is concentrated on its engine, chassis and body, so that it achieves its extraordinary performance by combining formidable power with lightness of construction.

Saving weight is a process in which shaving a few pounds, even ounces, in many, many areas of a car's specification adds up to a very significant whole. While racing car designers always have weight-saving high on their list of priorities, never before has lightness been so ruthlessly pursued in the design of a road car. The result is that the F40 is a featherweight by supercar standards, and therein lies much of its dynamic brilliance. Weighing just 2425lb (1100kg), little more than a ton, the F40 undercuts the Porsche 959 by 772lb (350kg) and the Testarossa by 895lb (406kg). No wonder it flies.

ENGINE
Unequalled on a road car
No other road car has ever been powered by a more formidable engine than the F40's twin-turbocharged 3-litre V8. Other engines have more cylinders and larger capacities, but the Ferrari unit beats everything – even the Porsche 959's twin-turbo flat-6 – in terms of outright power. It develops 478bhp at 7000rpm (the 959 manages 450bhp at 6500rpm) and 425lb ft of torque at 4000rpm (369lb ft at 5500rpm for the 959). As well as packing a bigger punch than its only conceivable rival, the F40 delivers over a much wider range. It also marks a big advance over its predecessor, the GTO; in terms of specific power, the F40 achieves 163bhp per litre compared with the 400bhp GTO's 140bhp per litre.

Designated type F120A, the F40's engine is distantly related to Ferrari's standard V8 found in the 328GTB/GTS (and the 348 which succeeded this model late in 1989), Mondial and Lancia Thema 8.32. This 'mass-production' engine dates back to 1973, when it was introduced in the 308GT4 as Ferrari's first road-going V8. The F40's engine is mounted longitudinally behind the passenger cabin and drives the rear wheels only. Its cylinder banks are angled at the classic 90°. As is Ferrari's normal practice, its crankcase, cylinder block and heads are made of aluminium/silicon alloy (Silumin) cast in the factory's own foundry. Aluminium cylinder liners, their working surfaces hardened with nickel/silicon alloy (Nikasil), are shrink-fitted. An 82mm bore and 69.5mm stroke (3.23 × 2.74in.) give a displacement of 2936.24cc; having such 'over-square' cylinder dimensions (bore:stroke ratio is 1.17:1) reduces piston speed and enables larger valves to be used, a combination which helps volumetric efficiency.

The crankshaft, a beautiful piece of sculpture in hardened and tempered steel, is machined from the solid and counter-balanced. It runs in five main bearings, with con rods connected in pairs through thinwall-type bearings made of silver/cadmium alloy in the interests of high-speed durability. A special feature of the crankshaft is its enlarged lubrication passages to cope with racing conditions, while track experience has also led to the pistons (which are machined to a shape giving pronounced 'squish' effect) having internal cooling by means of jets of oil. The compression ratio is 7.7:1.

Four valves per cylinder are actuated by two overhead camshafts on each bank, the inlet camshafts set above the exhaust ones. Each pair of camshafts is driven by a toothed rubber belt,

Below: F40's business end in all its glory under lift-up tail. Notice radiators behind rear wheels for gearbox oil (left) and engine oil (right), transverse exhaust silencer, heat shielding around exhaust and turbos, angled intercoolers and elegant manifolding above engine.

F40 3-LITRE V-8 ENGINE

Right: F40's Type F120A is ultimately derived from Ferrari's mainstream 90° V8 – first road-going engine of this configuration – launched in 1973, and still company's bread and butter unit today. F40's engine displaces 2936cc and has two overhead camshafts per bank.

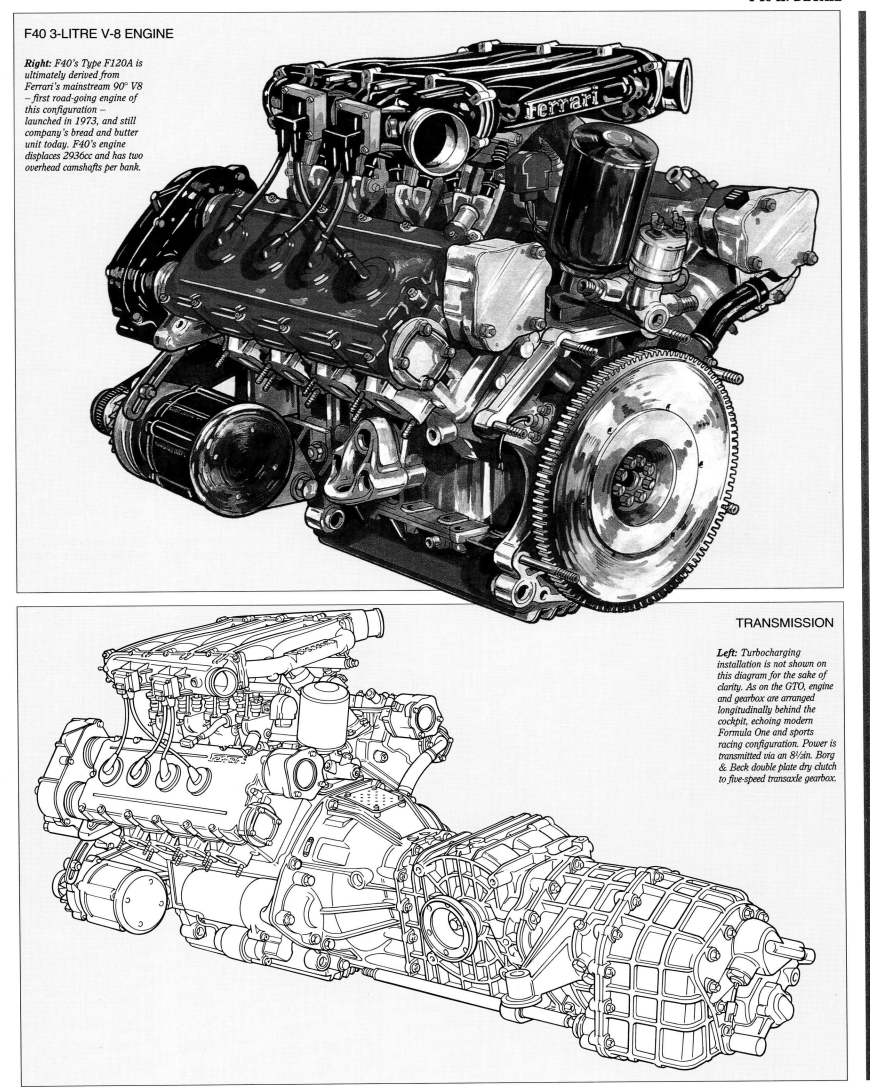

TRANSMISSION

Left: Turbocharging installation is not shown on this diagram for the sake of clarity. As on the GTO, engine and gearbox are arranged longitudinally behind the cockpit, echoing modern Formula One and sports racing configuration. Power is transmitted via an 8½in. Borg & Beck double plate dry clutch to five-speed transaxle gearbox.

VALVE GEAR

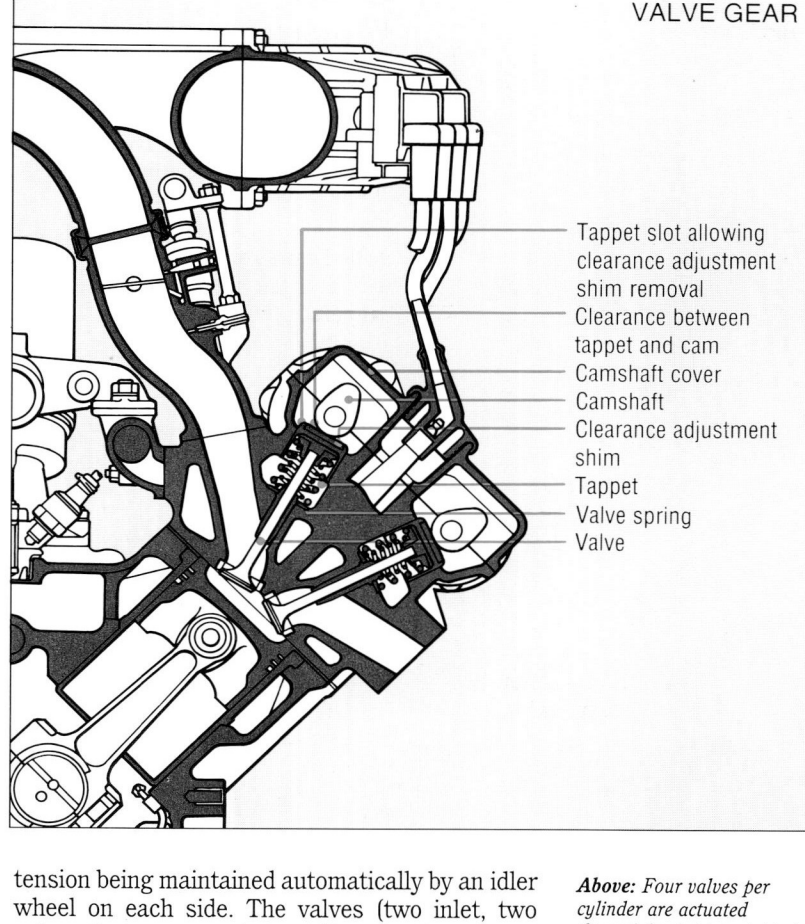

- Tappet slot allowing clearance adjustment shim removal
- Clearance between tappet and cam
- Camshaft cover
- Camshaft
- Clearance adjustment shim
- Tappet
- Valve spring
- Valve

tension being maintained automatically by an idler wheel on each side. The valves (two inlet, two exhaust) are arranged at a 46° angle; the exhaust valves borrow racing and aviation technology in being hollow, and sodium-filled, to assist heat dispersion. The valves are operated through bucket-type tappets with shims inserted to obtain the specified clearances of 0.20–0.25mm for inlets and 0.35–0.40mm for exhausts. These shims vary in thickness from 3.25mm to 4.60mm (in 0.05mm stages) and have hardened surfaces. Timing data

Above: Four valves per cylinder are actuated through bucket-type tappets by two overhead camshafts, the inlet camshaft being situated above the exhaust one.

Below: Two gear-driven pulleys close to the crankshaft carry toothed rubber belts, one per bank of cylinders, to drive the camshafts.

LAYOUT OF CAMSHAFT DRIVE

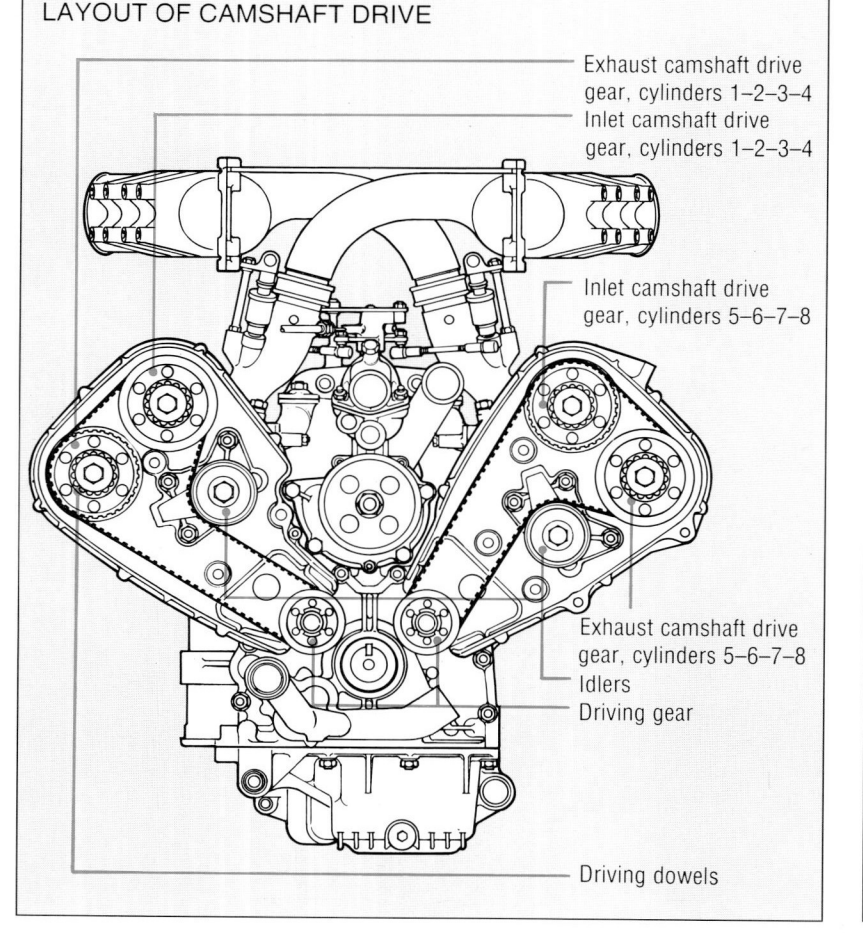

- Exhaust camshaft drive gear, cylinders 1–2–3–4
- Inlet camshaft drive gear, cylinders 1–2–3–4
- Inlet camshaft drive gear, cylinders 5–6–7–8
- Exhaust camshaft drive gear, cylinders 5–6–7–8
- Idlers
- Driving gear
- Driving dowels

FERRARI F40
Specifications

Engine	Configuration	V8, cylinder banks angled at 90°, mounted behind cockpit, type F120A
	Construction	All-alloy
	Capacity	2936.24cc (179.18cu.in.)
	Bore	82.0mm (3.23in.)
	Stroke	69.5mm (2.74in.)
	Compression ratio	7.7:1
	Main bearings	Five
	Max. engine speed	7750rpm
	Maximum power	478bhp (351.5kW) @ 7000rpm
	Specific power	162.8bhp/litre (119.7kW/litre)
	Maximum torque	425lb ft (577Nm) @ 4000rpm
	Valve gear	Four valves per cylinder, driven by two overhead camshafts (one intake, one exhaust) per bank
	Valve inclination	46° apart
	Camshaft drive	Toothed rubber belts
	Intake timing	Opens 16° BTDC, closes 48° ABDC
	Exhaust timing	Opens 54° BBDC, closes 10° ATDC
Turbocharging	Type	Two IHI RHB 53LW turbochargers

		(one per bank) with air-to-air intercoolers and wastegate
	Max. boost pressure	1.1bar
Cooling	Type	Closed-circuit water-cooled
	Radiator	Single front-mounted aluminium radiator carrying two thermostatically controlled electric fans switching in at 84°C, switching out at 75°C
	Capacity	3.74 gallons (17 litres) of water/antifreeze mixture pressurised at 1.1kg/cm². (15.7psi)
Fuel system	Type	Two Weber-Marelli integral ignition-injection systems (one per bank)
	Fuel delivery	Two electric pumps
	Fuel capacity	Two rubberised textile tanks totalling 26.4 gallons (120 litres) plus 4.4 gallon (20 litres) reserve
	Fuel grade	Four-star (98–100 octane)
Electrics	Ignition system	Two Weber-Marelli integral ignition-injection systems (one per bank)
	Spark plugs	Champion G61
	Plug size	0.40 × 0.04in. (10 × 1mm)
	Plug gap	0.02 × 0.024in. (0.5mm–0.6mm)
	Coils	Four
	Alternator	Bosch 105A
	Battery	12V/60Ah
	Starter motor	Bosch
Lubrication	Type	Dry sump system with separate oil tank and thermostatically regulated cooler, scavenge pump and pressure pump
	Oil capacity	17.6 pints (10.0 litres)
	Idle oil pressure	4.5kg/cm² (64.0psi)
	Max. oil pressure	6.5kg/cm² (92.5psi)
	Max. oil temperature	130°C
	Recommended oil	Agip Sint 2000 SAE 10W40
Transmission	Gearbox	Five-speed in unit with final drive, all-synchromesh, driving rear wheels, fitted with oil cooler
	Oil capacity	1.1 gallons (5 litres)
	Recommended oil	Agip Rotra MP SAE 80W90
	First gear	2.769:1
	Second gear	1.722:1
	Third gear	1.227:1
	Fourth gear	0.962:1
	Fifth gear	0.766:1
	Reverse ratio	2.461:1
	Final drive	Hypoid bevel gears with self-locking differential
	Final drive ratio	2.727:1
	Clutch	Borg & Beck dry double-plate, hydraulically actuated
Suspension	Front	Independent by double wishbones, coil springs, Koni 82–8322 shock absorbers, anti-roll bar, rubber bump and rebound blocks
	Rear	Independent by double wishbones, coil springs, Koni 82–8325 shock absorbers, anti-roll bar, rubber bump and rebound blocks
Steering	Type	Rack and pinion, symmetrical steering rods
	Ratio	2.89 turns lock to lock
	Turning circle	38.1ft (11.6m)

Brakes	System	Hydraulic without servo assistance, independent circuits front and rear
	Front	12.9in. (330mm) ventilated and drilled cast-iron/aluminium discs, with four-pot aluminium trailing calipers
	Rear	12.9in. (330mm) ventilated and drilled cast-iron/aluminium discs, with four-pot aluminium leading calipers
	Pads	Pagid RS4–2
	Handbrake	Cable-operated to separate rear disc calipers
Wheels/tyres	Front rims	Speedline five-spoke alloy split-rims, 8K × 17in.
	Front tyres	245/40 ZR 17 (Pirelli P Zero, Bridgestone RE71, Goodyear Eagle GSA or Michelin MXX)
	Front pressure	2.5–2.8bar (36–40psi)
	Front camber	−1°10′ to −1°30′
	Front toe-in	0.06–0.1in. (1.5–2.5mm)
	Front caster	5°10′–5°20′
	Rear rims	Speedline five-spoke alloy split-rims, 13K × 17in.
	Rear tyres	335/35 ZR 17 (Pirelli P Zero, Bridgestone RE71, Goodyear Eagle GSA or Michelin MXX)
	Rear pressure	2.5–2.8bar (36–40psi)
	Rear camber	−1°0′ to −1°20′
	Rear toe-in	0.1 × 0.14in. (2.5–3.5mm)
Structure	Chassis	Tubular steel cell, supplemented by composite panels (carbonfibre/Kevlar weave) bonded with structural adhesive
	Body	Panels in composite materials (glassfibre, carbonfibre, Kevlar)
Dimensions	Length	171.6in. (4358mm)
	Width	77.6in. (1970mm)
	Height	44.3in. (1124mm)
	Wheelbase	96.5in. (2450mm)
	Front track	62.8in. (1594mm)
	Rear track	63.2in. (1606mm)
	Kerb weight	2425lb (1100kg)
Performance[1]	Maximum speed	201.3mph (324kph)
	0–100kph (62.1mph)	4.1sec
	0–200kph (124.3mph)	11.0sec
	Standing kilometre	20.9sec
	0–400m	11.9sec
Performance[2]	0–30mph (48kph)	2.2sec
	0–40mph (64kph)	2.7sec
	0–50mph (80kph)	3.3sec
	0–60mph (97kph)	4.5sec
	0–70mph (113kph)	5.3sec
	0–80mph (129kph)	6.1sec
	0–90mph (145kph)	7.2sec
	0–100mph (161kph)	8.8sec
	0–110mph (177kph)	10.0sec
	0–120mph (193kph)	11.5sec
	0–130mph (209kph)	13.6sec
	0–140mph (225kph)	16.0sec
	0–150mph (241kph)	18.5sec
Consumption	Urban cycle	15.35mpg
	At 56mph (90kph)	32.85mpg
	At 75mph (120kph)	27.43mpg

[1] Official Ferrari performance figures.
[2] Performance figures quoted in *Autocar & Motor*, 11 January 1989.

is as follows: inlets open 16° before top dead centre (BTDC) and close 48° after bottom dead centre (ABDC); exhausts open 54° before bottom dead centre (BBDC) and close 10° after top dead centre (ATDC). The duration of the intake is 250° and of the exhaust 248°, with a 27° overlap.

Unlike mainstream V8 Ferraris, lubrication follows racing practice in using a dry sump system with two gear-type pumps. The scavenge pump draws oil from the sump, sends it to the Setrab oil cooler (mounted behind the car's right-hand rear wheel), and then to the oil tank (sited near the cockpit bulkhead); a thermostat prevents oil from passing through to the oil cooler until it has reached a temperature of 90°C. A delivery pump draws oil from the tank and sends it under pressure to the engine's rotating parts. Normal oil pressure is 82–97psi (5.5–6.5bar) at 6000rpm, and around 67psi (4.5bar) at idle. A crankcase emission control system is used to draw off unwanted oil vapours. An outlet from each cylinder head leads to the oil tank where vapour condenses to rejoin the oil supply.

The cooling system is laid out traditionally, with a single aluminium radiator cooled by twin electric fans sited at the front of the car. Coolant is fed to and from the engine via two tubes passing through the passenger cabin in the channel between the seats, while a smaller return tube leads to the expansion tank in the engine bay. This is a conventional closed-circuit system filled with 3.74 gallons (17 litres) of water/antifreeze mixture pressurised at 15psi, the coolant being circulated by a centrifugal water pump driven by a vee-belt from the crankshaft nose. The expansion tank, incorporating a pressure-relief valve in the filler cap, takes up the surplus caused by the coolant increasing in volume and pressure when it heats up. A thermostat triggers the electric fans when

coolant temperature reaches 84°C and switches them off again below 75°C.

One of the most advanced features of the F40's engine is its Weber-Marelli IAW centralised ignition-injection, comprising two separate systems, one for each bank of cylinders. This electronic engine management system owes much of its technology to Formula One experience. Each of these integral ignition and fuel injection systems is controlled by a microprocessor electronic management unit, a box the size of a car radio attached to the engine/cockpit bulkhead. Each cylinder is fed by two electro-magnetic injectors, and each intake line – and therefore each cylinder – has an individually governed throttle valve. The management box meters the amount of fuel to be sent to the injectors according to engine speed and the position of the throttle valves, but at the same time it can take account of other parameters – boost pressure, water temperature, air temperature, battery voltage and detonation – to optimise engine performance (by adjusting the quantity of fuel and degree of ignition advance) under all operating conditions.

A range of sensors supplies the mass of data which the two electronic management boxes require to control the fuel injection so precisely. Information is received on the position of the throttle valves (via a potentiometer located on the rear of the throttle valve body), engine rpm, air temperature and absolute pressure, engine temperature (by means of a water temperature sensor), engine timing (a stroke sensor is located on the inlet timing camshaft of one cylinder bank) and the onset of detonation (a sensor recognises the approach of the detonation limit). The management unit enriches the mixture for cold starting and adds an enrichment factor for maximum power at full throttle openings. Cold running is

further eased by an accelerated idling actuator which acts on the throttle valve opening control lever, in response to a signal from the left-hand management unit, to raise idling speed.

The ignition part of this sophisticated Weber-Marelli package incorporates two high-energy coils for each bank of cylinders; each coil supplies the ignition to two cylinders in a pattern whereby one cylinder is fired when the other is in the exhaust phase. Two power modules for each bank determine the precise moment of coil charging and discharging – this is a completely static system, with no distributors.

The two foam-filled rubberised textile fuel tanks borrow Formula One and aviation technology to provide the best safeguard against fire; tanks of this specification have never before been used on a production road car. They have been homologated for use in competition, so the only change necessary when racing an F40 is to replace the standard filler cap with the rapid filling type used on endurance sports prototypes. These inter-linked tanks are sited on each side of the car behind the passenger compartment and have a capacity totalling 30.8 gallons (140 litres), 4.4 gallons (20 litres) of which is a reserve. Fuel is drawn from the tanks by two electric pumps and sent to the injectors via two filters and two pressure regulators.

Two Japanese water-cooled IHI RHB 53 LW turbochargers (again, one system per bank) provide the turbocharging. The four-into-one exhaust manifolds from each cylinder bank direct exhaust gases to the two turbines, which turn coaxially

Below: A special feature of the F40's engine is its Weber-Marelli microprocessor management system controlling fuel injection and ignition. Each bank of cylinders has a separate system which uses a range of sensors to meter the amount of fuel supplied to the injectors.

IGNITION-INJECTION SYSTEM

Air temperature sensor
Ignition coil
Absolute air pressure sensor
Ignition and injection electronic management unit
Fuel pressure regulator
Socket for connecting diagnostic equipment
Excessive pressure warning light
Detonation sensor
Rev counter
Socket for connecting diagnostic equipment
Fuel pressure regulator
Accelerated idling actuator electronic control unit
Ignition and injection electronic management unit
Fuel pump

Power module
Boost pressure control valve
Water temperature sensor
Stroke sensor
Electrically-powered injector
Engine speed sensor
Throttle valve opening potentiometer
Accelerated idling actuator
Throttle valve opening potentiometer
Engine speed sensor
Electrically-powered injector
Stroke sensor
Air temperature sensor
Ignition coil
Power module
Absolute air pressure sensor

LUBRICATION

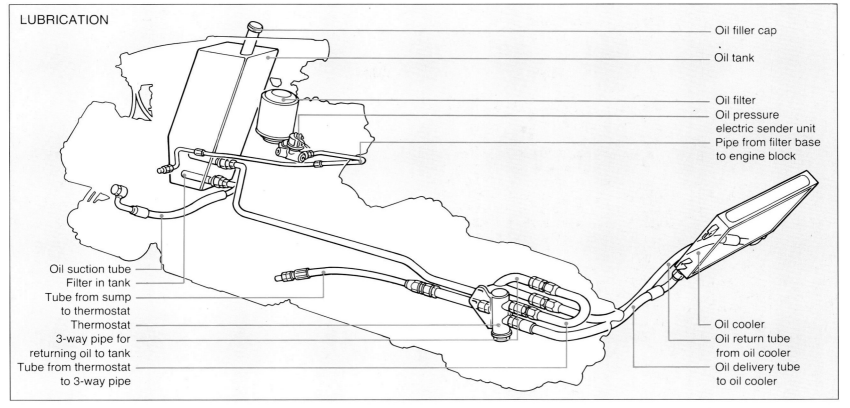

Oil filler cap

Oil tank

Oil filter
Oil pressure electric sender unit
Pipe from filter base to engine block

Oil suction tube
Filter in tank
Tube from sump to thermostat
Thermostat
3-way pipe for returning oil to tank
Tube from thermostat to 3-way pipe

Oil cooler
Oil return tube from oil cooler
Oil delivery tube to oil cooler

TURBOCHARGING SYSTEM

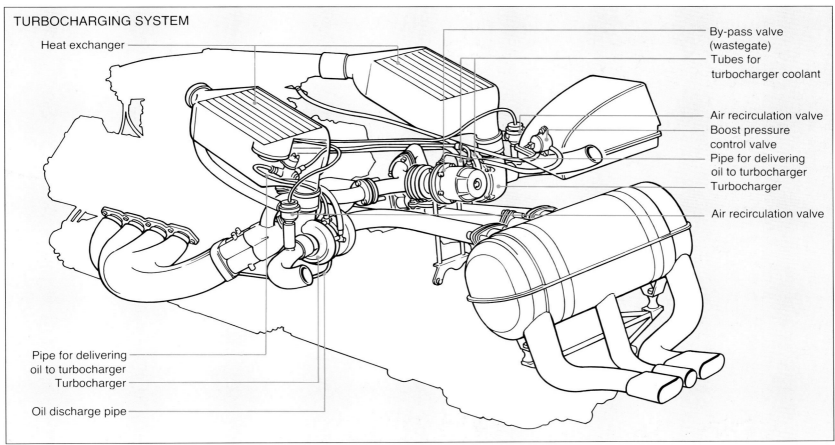

Heat exchanger

By-pass valve (wastegate)
Tubes for turbocharger coolant

Air recirculation valve
Boost pressure control valve
Pipe for delivering oil to turbocharger
Turbocharger

Air recirculation valve

Pipe for delivering oil to turbocharger
Turbocharger

Oil discharge pipe

with centrifugal compressors. The compressed air is sent through two German Behr air-to-air heat exchangers, or intercoolers, in order that its temperature is lowered before it reaches the inlet plenum chambers. Each of the two turbocharging systems supplies the opposite bank of cylinders; the left-hand compressor, therefore, supplies the right-hand bank of cylinders, and vice versa. Lubrication and cooling for the turbochargers is incorporated into the engine's main systems: the shaft linking the compressor and turbine is lubricated by engine oil under pressure, while the turbocharger bearing housing is cooled by the engine coolant.

A single wastegate opens to bypass exhaust

Top: Dry sump lubrication system, with oil tank beside engine and oil cooler in car's tail. Above: Two separate turbocharging systems –

with Japanese turbos and air-to-air intercoolers – linked to single wastegate releasing excess gas through central exhaust.

gases away from the turbines when boost pressure reaches 1.1bar, directing the excess instead through the central pipe of the three exhausts which emerge from the tail of the car. The wastegate is operated by a solenoid valve according to engine speed and the absolute pressure in the intake plenum chamber. The system is set so that the optimum boost for the best performance is obtained at any engine speed, with maximum boost coinciding with the peak of the torque curve.

The turbocharging installation is also designed to keep throttle lag – the perennial disadvantage of forced induction – to a minimum. One of the features which contributes to reducing lag is a charge air recirculation valve, which limits the drop in compressor rotor speed when the throttle is lifted. Without this device, shutting off the throttle valves would create back pressure which would slow down the compressor rotors, giving rise to pronounced throttle lag upon subsequent acceleration. The charge air recirculation valve, however, operates when a depression is detected in the inlet manifold, opening a recirculation route between the delivery and intake sides of the compressor to limit the drop in rotor speed. As a

TRANSMISSION CROSS SECTION

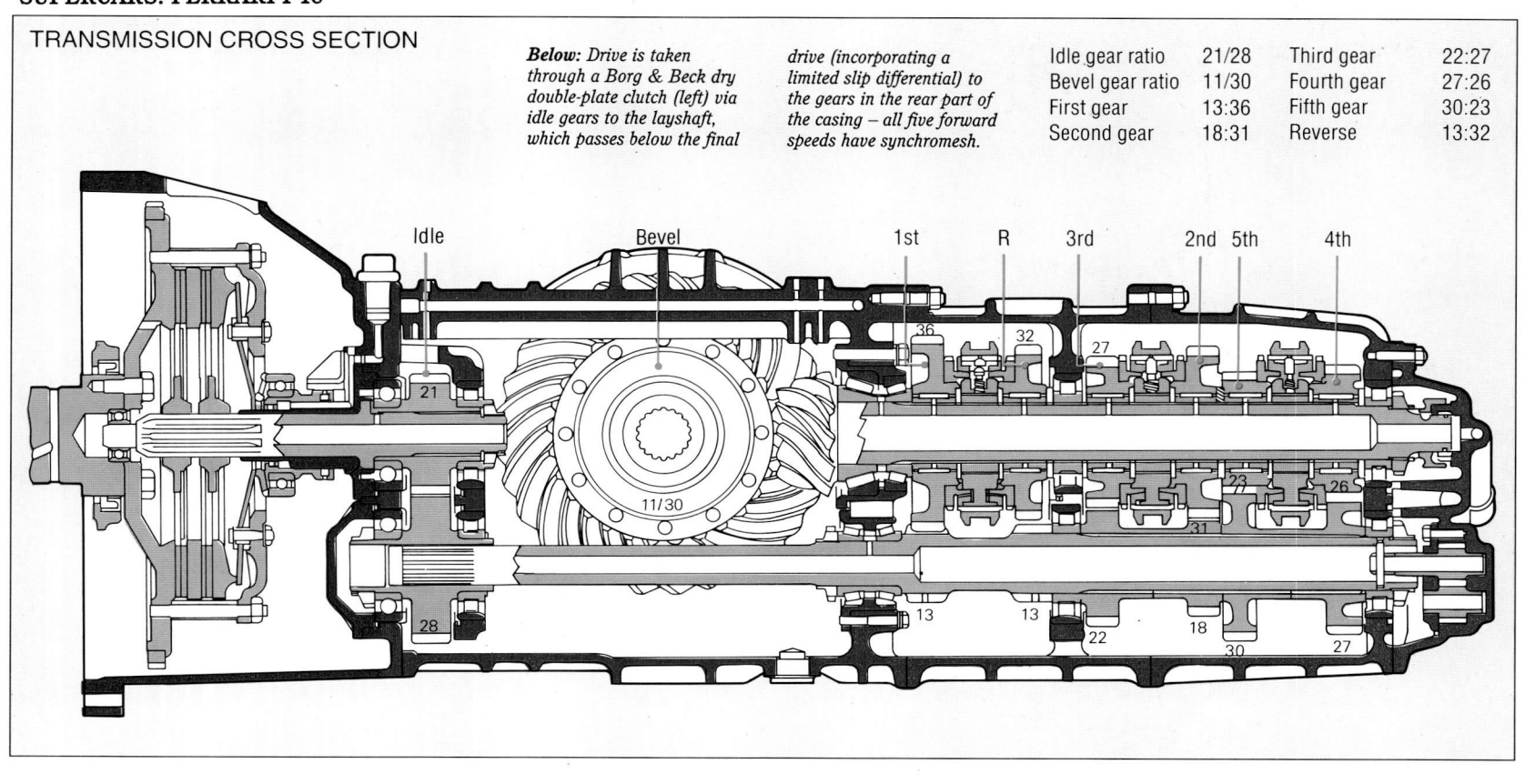

Below: Drive is taken through a Borg & Beck dry double-plate clutch (left) via idle gears to the layshaft, which passes below the final *drive (incorporating a limited slip differential) to the gears in the rear part of the casing – all five forward speeds have synchromesh.*

Idle gear ratio	21:28	Third gear	22:27
Bevel gear ratio	11/30	Fourth gear	27:26
First gear	13:36	Fifth gear	30:23
Second gear	18:31	Reverse	13:32

result, quicker response is available when acceleration is demanded once again by the driver.

TRANSMISSION
Strength is the key
Drive is transmitted to the rear wheels through a Ferrari-manufactured five-speed gearbox positioned behind the engine and in line with it. The normal specification gearbox has synchromesh on all five forward speeds, but a racing-type 'crash' gearbox, without synchromesh, can be chosen by a customer planning to run his car in competition. The gearbox also contains the crown wheel and pinion and limited slip differential.

There are pairs of gears for each speed on the layshaft and output shaft, the first three gears being reduction ratios, fourth and fifth overdrive ratios. The ratios are 2.769:1 (first), 1.722:1 (second), 1.227:1 (third), 0.962:1 (fourth) and

0.766:1 (fifth); reverse ratio is 2.461:1. A pair of bevel gears transmit the power to the differential. To cope with the transmission's great lubrication demands, a Setrab oil cooler is included in the system, mounted behind the left-hand rear wheel.

The clutch is a Borg & Beck 8½in. dry double-plate unit with a shock-absorbing hub, a diaphragm spring and hydraulic actuation.

SUSPENSION AND STEERING
Designed for handling perfection
The F40's suspension, like so many other aspects of the car's specification, has benefited from

Below: Two 26.4 gallon fuel tanks made of rubberised textile (and filled with foam) use aviation and racing technology to reduce fire *risk. The tanks may be filled separately, but are linked so that the paired fuel pumps draw only from the tank on the left-hand side.*

racing experience in using expensive strengthened steels which offer great rigidity and lightness.

Independent at front and rear, the suspension uses quadrilateral upper and lower wishbones (made of welded tubular steel) anchored through rubber bushes to the chassis at their wide-based ends, and to cast alloy uprights at the narrow ends. Double-acting Koni shock absorbers enclosed by coil springs operate directly between the uprights and the chassis, without any interposed levers. Each front shock absorber (Koni 82-8322) is mounted to the base of its upright and meets the chassis at a point between the upper wishbone arms. Each rear shock absorber (Koni 82-8325) rises from the top of its upright to attach to a much higher point on the chassis. Rubber bushes are fitted at the top to act as bump stops, and internal resilient bushes form the rebound stops at the bottom. Anti-roll bars are fitted at each end.

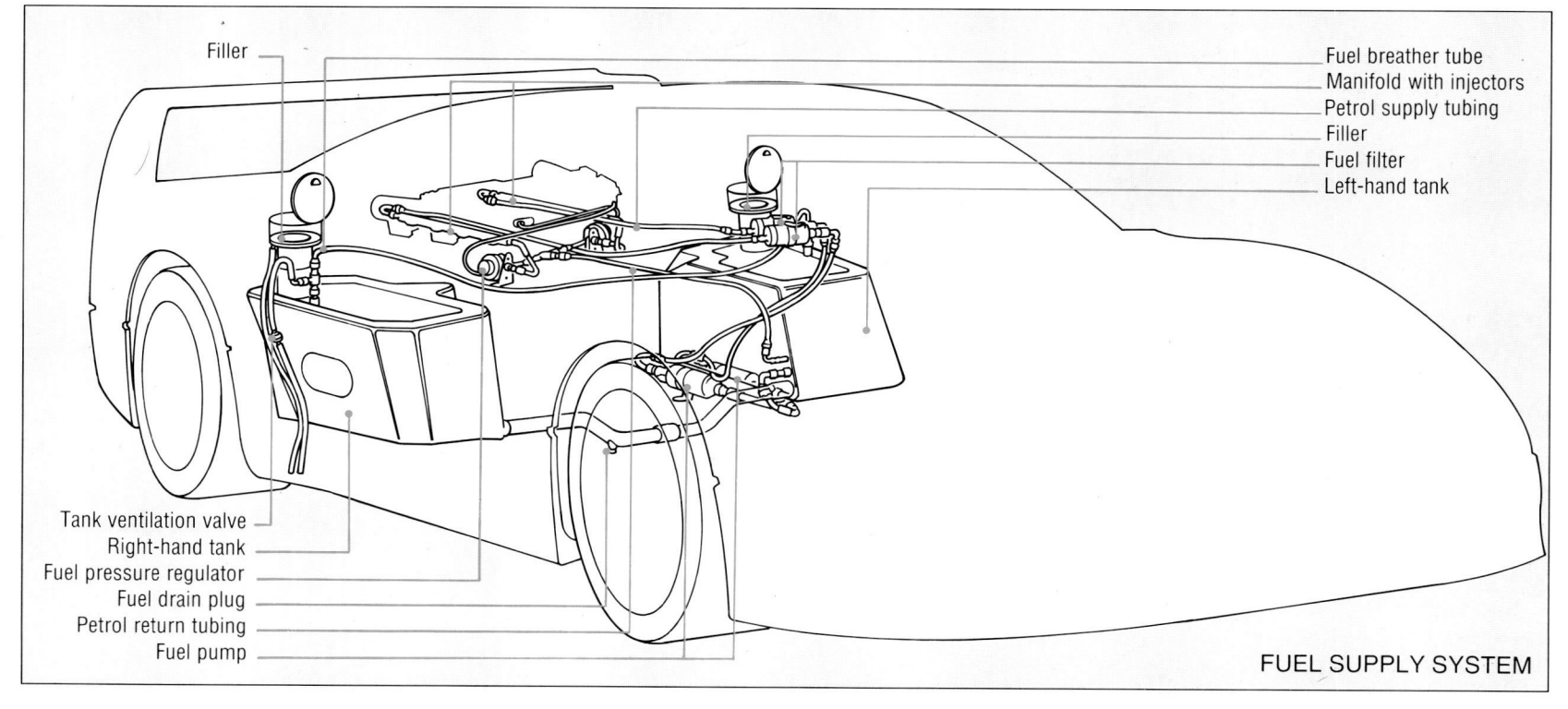

FUEL SUPPLY SYSTEM

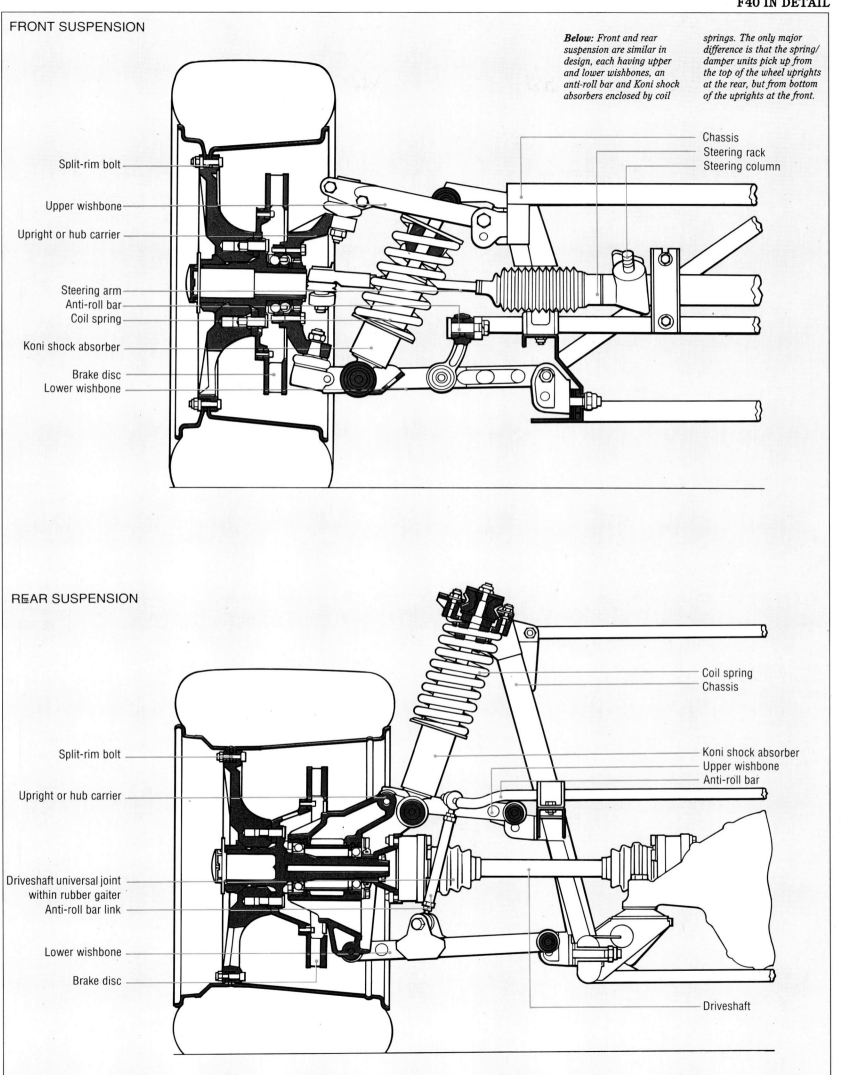

FRONT SUSPENSION

Below: Front and rear suspension are similar in design, each having upper and lower wishbones, an anti-roll bar and Koni shock absorbers enclosed by coil springs. The only major difference is that the spring/damper units pick up from the top of the wheel uprights at the rear, but from bottom of the uprights at the front.

Split-rim bolt

Upper wishbone

Upright or hub carrier

Steering arm
Anti-roll bar
Coil spring

Koni shock absorber

Brake disc
Lower wishbone

Chassis
Steering rack
Steering column

REAR SUSPENSION

Coil spring
Chassis

Koni shock absorber
Upper wishbone
Anti-roll bar

Split-rim bolt

Upright or hub carrier

Driveshaft universal joint within rubber gaiter
Anti-roll bar link

Lower wishbone

Brake disc

Driveshaft

Ferrari has always intended that the F40's suspension should include a ride height adjustment facility giving three positions: high for manoeuvring, normal for moderate speed and low for high speed. The intention is that the normal ride height of 4.9in. (125mm) is automatically reduced by 0.8in. (20mm) at speeds above 120kph (75mph) to give better aerodynamic stability. By pushing a switch on the fascia, the driver would also be able to raise the normal ground clearance by 1in. (25mm) when manoeuvring over bumps.

The changes in height are achieved by a hydraulic system built into the shock absorbers. Powered by an electrically driven pump, valves

*Below: Conventional closed-circuit cooling system uses single front-mounted aluminium radiator and two electric fans. **Bottom:***

Brakes are powerful, but no servo assistance is needed: 12.9in. ventilated discs have aluminium centres faced with cast-iron friction surfaces.

transfer hydraulic fluid according to commands from a sensor measuring speed. A safeguard is built in to avoid frequent height changes when speed hovers around the 120kph point. As this is written, however, the system has yet to be perfected for production, so the option will be available only to later F40 customers. According to Maurizio Manfredini of the Experimental Department, the lowest ride height setting adds 2kph to the F40's top speed.

A conventional rack and pinion arrangement looks after the steering. Despite the immense size of the front wheels, steering effort is so relatively low that no power assistance is necessary. The rack is geared to give a reasonably 'quick' ratio of 2.89 turns from lock to lock, while the turning circle is 38.1ft (11.6m). The collapsible steering column incorporates two universal joints between the fixed steering wheel and the pinion.

BRAKES
Enormous stopping power

In order to produce a braking system capable of arresting the F40 from its maximum speed, Ferrari has used its Formula One experience (from the days before carbonfibre brake discs became *de rigueur*) to develop special discs for the car in conjunction with Brembo. Apart from their enormous 12.9in. (330mm) diameter, the discs have benefited from very close attention to lightness, since minimal unsprung weight is desirable for stable braking. As a result, each disc has an aluminium core sandwiched by the cast-iron friction surfaces. As well as having the usual lateral ventilation passages, the discs are drilled to help dissipate heat during the heavy use imposed by racing conditions. Brembo four-piston aluminium calipers carrying Pagid RS4-2 pads are fitted to each disc.

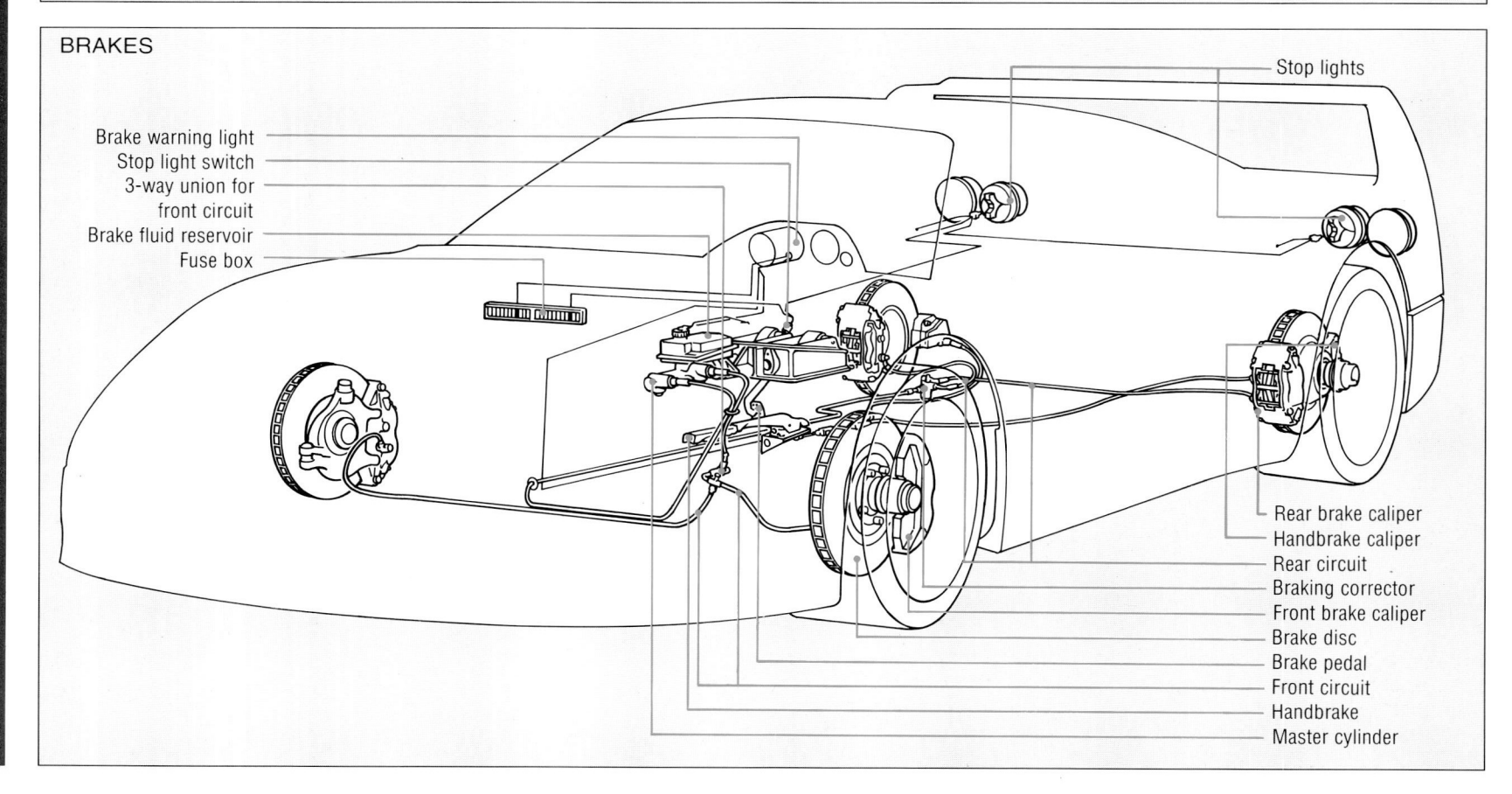

COOLING SYSTEM

Return tube to expansion tank
Radiator
Electric fans
Thermal contact for operating fans

Expansion tank
Thermostat body
Air bleed screw

BRAKES

Brake warning light
Stop light switch
3-way union for front circuit
Brake fluid reservoir
Fuse box

Stop lights

Rear brake caliper
Handbrake caliper
Rear circuit
Braking corrector
Front brake caliper
Brake disc
Brake pedal
Front circuit
Handbrake
Master cylinder

Above: Koni shock absorbers with co-axial coil springs are used at all four corners – those at the front pick up from the bottom of *the upright, those at the back (as shown here) from the top of the upright. The duct (with paper filter) leads to turbo compressor.*

Unusually for a road car, the F40 has no servo assistance to lighten pedal loads, simply because the pressure required without servo was found to be acceptable. Ferrari claims that a force of 42kg (92.6lb) will produce 1g deceleration – many cars *with* servo assistance require pressure of a similar order.

Separate hydraulic circuits are used for the front and rear brakes so that emergency braking is still possible in the event of one circuit failing. Racing-type flexible brake pipes are used, so no changes to the system need to be made for competition. The cable handbrake operates through separate calipers on the rear discs.

WHEELS AND TYRES
Close to racing standards
While the F40's Speedline alloy wheels have Ferrari's traditional bold five-spoke pattern, the similarity with Maranello's other models goes no further; the F40 has wheels and tyres of massive width. The front rims are 8J × 17in., the rear rims 13J × 17in.; these are racing-type split rims, the two sections of each rim being mated by twenty-five studs. Racing practice also extends to the means of wheel location, for each rim carries a single octagonal locking nut and a securing pin. Wheel nuts must be tightened with a torque wrench to 65kgm.

F40s are supplied with one of four brands of tyre – Pirelli P Zero, Bridgestone RE71, Goodyear Eagle GSA or Michelin MXX. Pirelli P Zeros are most commonly used. The 335/35 ZR 17 rear tyres are the largest fitted to any production car,

and in width are only slightly narrower than Formula One or sports prototype wear. Since the front tyres do not have to transmit power and bear less of the weight distribution, they are much narrower; Pirellis and Bridgestones are 245/40 ZR 17, Goodyears and Michelins 235/45 ZR 17.

No spare wheel is fitted to the F40, but a special Agip tyre sealant bottle is supplied instead. This substance can provide enough pressure in an emergency – if a puncture is not too severe – for the car to be driven at speeds up to 150kph (93mph), but it cannot cope with large holes or gashes.

CHASSIS
Strength with lightness
Apart from the engine's sophistication, the most technologically advanced part of the F40's specification is its chassis. Like other Ferraris, the F40 has a basic tubular steel space-frame structure, but on to this are bonded composite panels to lend extra rigidity. The complete composite/steel structure weighs 20 per cent less than a conventional chassis, yet Ferrari claims that strength and stiffness are improved by a factor of three.

The steel elements of the chassis form a passenger cell with front and rear extensions to provide mounting points for the engine/gearbox and front and rear suspension. Steel hoops within the windscreen pillars, across the roof and behind the passenger compartment are used to give roll-over strength. The sturdiest members are found on the floor of the chassis; large tubes run the length of the chassis at each side of the car, two

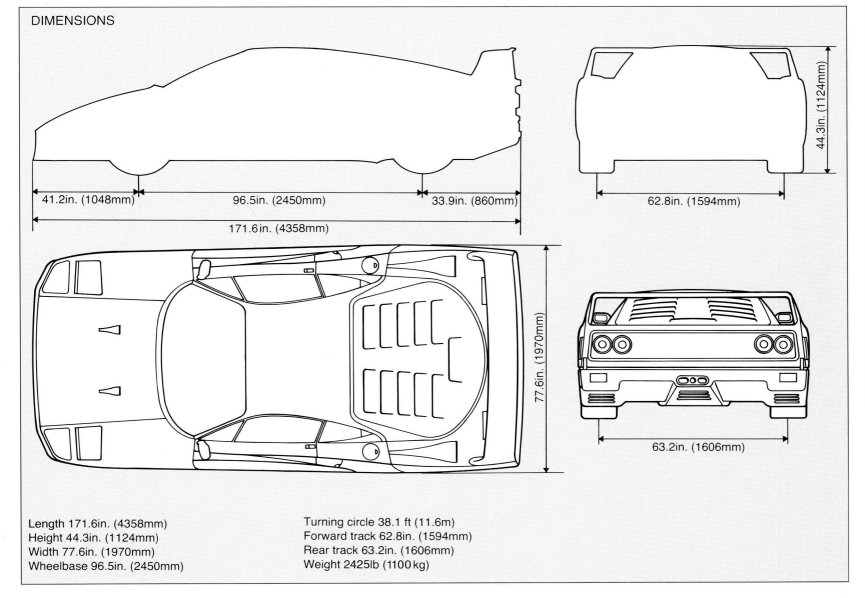

DIMENSIONS

41.2in. (1048mm) 96.5in. (2450mm) 33.9in. (860mm)

171.6in. (4358mm)

44.3in. (1124mm)

62.8in. (1594mm)

77.6in. (1970mm)

63.2in. (1606mm)

Length 171.6in. (4358mm)
Height 44.3in. (1124mm)
Width 77.6in. (1970mm)
Wheelbase 96.5in. (2450mm)

Turning circle 38.1 ft (11.6m)
Forward track 62.8in. (1594mm)
Rear track 63.2in. (1606mm)
Weight 2425lb (1100kg)

similar cross-member tubes link them along the lines of the front and rear bulkheads, and a third longitudinal tube runs up the centre of the chassis to join these cross-members. Square-section tubing provides most of the bracing added to this basic frame.

The composite panels glued to this steel frame with structural adhesive contain a variety of materials, depending upon their purpose. Most of the composites forming the floor and footwells, all visible from inside the car, are a weave of black carbonfibre and yellow Kevlar. Nomex is also a constituent of the pair of tapered joists lying at the base of the door openings, and of the bulkhead between the cockpit and the engine; this bulkhead, or firewall, is a fire-resistant panel which can be removed to give access to the front part of the engine. Two smaller panels situated either side of the firewall are made from honeycomb and aluminium.

BODY
Plastic sculpture

The F40's stunning shape is dictated entirely by aerodynamics. The Cd figure is 0.34, and the CdA – the product of the frontal area and the drag coefficient – is 0.63. Even though some mundane production cars are creeping below 0.30 Cd these days, the F40's figure is impressive considering the drag-inducing downforce aids needed to keep the car on the ground towards its maximum speed. Indeed, the massive rear wing is the most striking feature of the car. Its inverted aerofoil section generates considerable downforce which is balanced by the effect of the deep chin spoiler at the nose to keep the car stable at all speeds.

The prevailing impression of the F40's styling is that straight edges and flat surfaces feature more prominently than curves. The nose is broad and almost flat, apart from the slightly raised sections which run back over the wheels from the headlight area. The rear deck is similarly flat, tapering gently downwards almost to the horizontal underneath the wing. In profile the line of the

Below left: One of thirteen air intakes on an F40 – this one divides air to gearbox oil cooler and engine compartment (to help expel hot air). Below right: Weave of yellow Kevlar and black carbonfibre clearly visible on inner door skin – black cable releases door latch.

F40 CUTAWAY

Above: Every detail is visible in this splendid cutaway drawing. Notice how much of the engine has been exposed, right down to pistons, valves, spark plugs and fuel injectors. Differing colours of composite surfaces stand out on chassis floor, door skins, seat shells and rear bodywork. Double wishbone suspension, spring/damper unit and drilled disc brake are clearly visible at the rear. There are two signs that the artist based his work on photographs of an early prototype – a mirror is fitted to the driver's door and too many vents are shown on the rear window. Interestingly, a spare wheel is shown in the car's nose, although F40s are supplied with a puncture sealant bottle instead.

nose merges neatly into the windscreen, with barely a change in angle. Having such a stark vertical edge to the tail adds to the aggressive appearance, but this visual feature is necessary to create a smooth passage of air behind the car. The F40's central section is very similar in shape to the GTO and GTB/GTS models, with almost identical roof and door lines; even the windscreen is the same.

Myriad ducts and vents for air intakes and outlets puncture the F40's surface. There are thirteen intakes altogether, all bar the three at the nose having the conical NACA form which has been found to allow tidy ingress of air with minimal disruption to surface flow. Cut into the nose spoiler are three air intakes, the central one for the water radiator and the outer pair for cooling the front brakes. Two ducts two-thirds of the way back over the nose lead to the air-conditioning system.

The remaining eight ducts, four on each side,

Left: Interesting comparison shot with GTO shows how F40's nose plunges much lower to the ground – more power, better aerodynamics and lighter weight account for its 12mph top speed advantage. Cockpit sections are almost identical, and windscreen is the same on both.

CHASSIS

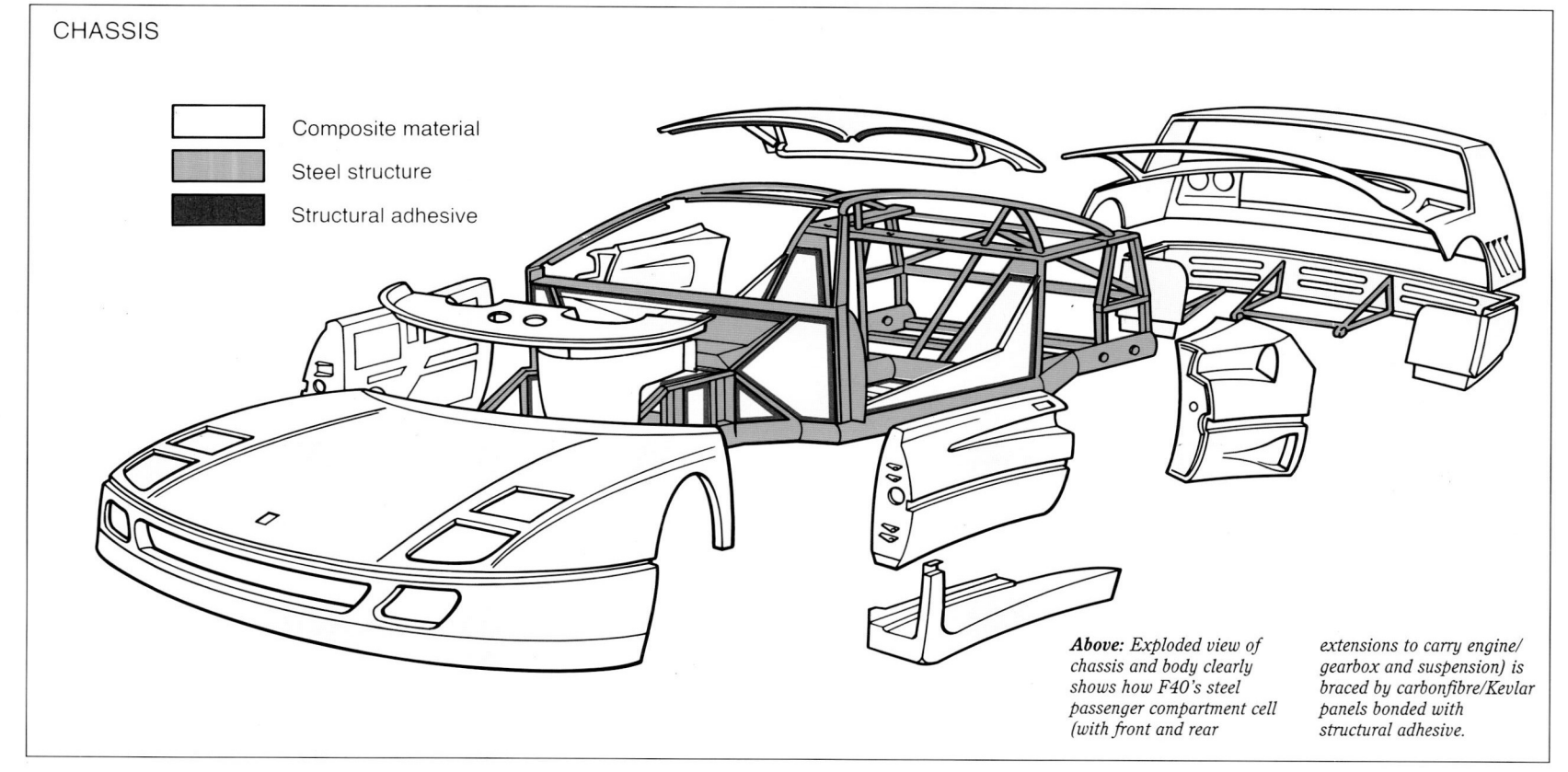

▢	Composite material
▨	Steel structure
▉	Structural adhesive

Above: Exploded view of chassis and body clearly shows how F40's steel passenger compartment cell (with front and rear extensions to carry engine/ gearbox and suspension) is braced by carbonfibre/Kevlar panels bonded with structural adhesive.

are clustered towards the tail of the car. The two behind the rear three-quarter windows supply air to the turbochargers. The large ducts along the tops of the doors lead to the intercoolers, while the smaller intakes below these direct cool air to the rear brakes. The other two ducts are positioned on the rear deck just ahead of the wing: the left-hand duct is divided in two, half leading to the gearbox oil cooler, half directly into the engine compartment to help expel hot air; the right-hand duct, which is not divided, leads to the engine oil cooler.

The F40's rear quarters are dominated by openings through which heat from the engine bay can be dispersed. The rear bodywork contains three slots on the flat surface beneath the rear aerofoil, a row of four further vertical slots behind the rear wheels, and a large opening filled with black gauze (which supports the tail lights) across the back. Even the plexiglass rear window contains eleven apertures, arranged in two rows of five with a single one in the centre.

With the exception of the flush-fitting windscreen, all the windows are made of Lexan plexiglass, in keeping with the weight-saving philosophy. The much criticised sliding side windows are fitted simply because these are the lightest and simplest solution, even if they are rather inelegant. A small plexiglass panel slides back in plastic runners, and is secured when shut by a plastic latch. Adverse comments from customers about these windows, however, led Ferrari to develop wind-up glass windows (and trimmed door inner skins) once the F40 was in production, so a buyer has been able to choose which type of window he prefers. The windscreen has to be laminated glass to give surface hardness and to withstand the impact of flying stones; the single wiper blade would scratch plexiglass. In the parked position the windscreen wiper is shielded from the air stream by a slight lip at the trailing edge of the nose section.

Of course, there is no unnecessary adornment to the F40's body; only the black strip insert running all round the car at knee level could be considered functionless trim. Badging is kept to a

minimum; a small traditional yellow badge is found on the nose, chromed 'Ferrari' script is positioned centrally on the upper surface of the tail, and the flanks bear Prancing Horse shields and 'Disegno di Pininfarina' inscriptions. The use of enamelled shield badges is significant, for this style is reserved for Ferraris designed for competition; all other current production Ferraris use the normal rectangular badge. The F40 motif is embossed only on the left-hand rear wing upright.

Above: Some say that these racing-type sliding side windows, made of Lexan plexiglass, take the lightness touch too far. They are prone to scratching, are difficult to use and look crudely manufactured – conventional wind-up glass windows can now be specified instead.

Two fuel fillers are located beneath flimsy flush-fitting composite flaps on the horizontal surface above the rear wheels. These fillers are exquisitely crafted in polished aluminium, with such attention to detail that the lockable caps carry Ferrari emblems. The door handles are little painted steel levers lying flush with the bodywork where it meets the side windows. Manually adjustable wing mirrors contained in body colour pods are mounted on the doors, although on the much-photographed prototypes the mirrors sprouted out from the front corners of the quarter-light windows.

Only twelve pieces – made from Kevlar, carbonfibre and glassfibre – are used to construct the body. The nose section is the largest single piece, and swings forward on mounting points up front when two clasps behind the front wheels are unlocked. The tail section is also a single piece embracing the entire upper deck, the wing supports, the upper half of the rear wheelarches and the cut-off tail panel (including the rear lights); again, this is opened by releasing two lockable clasps, the whole structure rising on hinges at the back of the roof. The wing itself is a separate moulding which is secured to each support by three recessed Allen bolts. The remaining panels are the roof, a small bib ahead of the windscreen, the rear under-valance, two doors, two fixed body sections ahead of the rear wheels and two side sill sections.

All of these body panels are quite astonishingly light; each door weighs 3.3lb (1.5kg), the nose section 39.6lb (18.0kg) and the tail section (including the wing) 48.5lb (22.0kg).

Above: Flimsy flap (made of composite) lifts to expose elegantly crafted lockable fuel filler, complete with Ferrari emblem. There is a fuel filler on each side for each of the two inter-linked 26.4 gallon tanks, which are made of rubberised textile and contain foam filling.

Below: Without any impression of scale, this could be an intricate model of an F40 – but it's the real thing. Nose-piece supports itself when open, tail section needs a stout prop. Massive 335/35 ZR 17 Pirelli P Zero tyres at the back have asymmetrical tread pattern.

LIGHTING
200mph in the dark?

The F40's comprehensive lighting at the front is housed in pop-up pods and behind glass panels containing heating elements. Raised by electric motors (with an over-riding hand-cranking device in case the motors fail), the pods contain Siem dipped and main beam 55w halogen headlights mounted in integral housings; the rectangular main beam lenses are inboard of the square dipped beams. The glassed-over recesses below these pods contain further Siem 55w square halogen lights for daytime flashing, and rectangular units with 5w pilot lights and 21w direction indicators.

At the rear, most of the lighting functions are arranged in two pairs of circular light units. The outer pair contain 21w reversing lights in the centre surrounded by 21w direction indicators, while the inner pair have a central reflector surrounded by 5w pilot and 21w stop lights. Two rectangular high-intensity 21w rear fog lights are mounted below these tail lights on the undervalance. Two 5w number plate lights are positioned under the top lip of the tail. Direction indicator repeaters (3w) are located ahead of the front wheel on each side of the car.

INTERIOR
The bare minimum

Expensive cars invariable cosset their occupants in surroundings of some luxury, but not an inch of leather, thick carpet or wood veneer is to be found in the F40. Sybaritic this Ferrari is not. The F40 may be one of the most expensive cars in the world, but when it comes to interior furnishings it cannot match up to even the most frugal base

Above left: Front view with headlight pods raised – separate dipped and main beam lights are contained in the pod, while daytime flashing lights are behind glass panel below. *Above right:* Elegant tail lights are same as those on all other Ferraris except Testarossa.

Below: Close-up of chassis floor shows how composite materials are used. The direction of the 'grain' and the proportion of Kevlar, carbonfibre and glassfibre used depend on the structural role of each panel – the green 'weld' lines are structural adhesive.

models produced behind the Iron Curtain. But then the spartan touch is all part of the F40's rationale; all the inessentials have been discarded.

The F40's interior is intentionally bare; no door trim, no carpet, no padding. Instead, the decor is predominantly of stark carbonfibre and Kevlar, with the composite weave of the chassis panels visible right across the floor, in the footwells and on the stout reinforcing beams either side of the seats. Soft fabrics are used only where they are strictly needed. Dark grey felt covers the simple fascia to provide a surface which deadens reflections in the windscreen, while the engine/cockpit bulkhead and the central tunnel (which shrouds the gear linkage and pipework between front-mounted ancillaries and engine bay) are also trimmed with this material. The thinly padded seat shells, again made of composite material, are trimmed with scarlet velour; the headlining is made of pale grey perforated plastic.

Since the only seat adjustment is fore/aft movement, three seat sizes are available to suit the build of the driver. The two seats have a pronounced 'wraparound' shape to keep the occupants in place. Two slots at shoulder level allow a four-point racing-type Sabelt safety harness to be fitted, although F40s are normally offered with conventional three-point inertia reel belts.

The doors are no more than skimpy Kevlar panels which serve to fill the openings. Each one is hollow, so that the inside surface of unfinished composite (comprised mainly of yellow Kevlar) can be seen within a red-painted frame forming the inner skin. The joins between door panels and windows are filled with black mastic. There are no interior door handles – just plastic-coated cables which are pulled to release the door latches.

Above: Seats are composite shells trimmed with thin padding and scarlet velour. They are superbly comfortable, with pronounced shoulder and waist bolsters to offer excellent support. This car has inertia reel safety belts, but four-point harnesses can be fitted.

Below: Cockpit is comfortable, but reduced to the bare minimum. Floor is bare composite (carbonfibre predominates to give a grey appearance); dark grey felt covers fascia, central tunnel and windscreen pillars. Relays and fuses live behind rectangular fascia panel.

The demands of lightness extend even to the pedals, all three being made of aluminium drilled with holes to save weight. The clutch and brake pedals are hinged from above, while the organ-pedal accelerator pivots from the floor alongside the central channel running back through the car.

The gear lever is quintessential Ferrari: just a purposeful shaft poking up from a six-bar gate of stainless steel, topped by a simple black knob etched in white with the gear pattern. The simple steering wheel, which has a black leather rim and

Below: Despite the weight of the system, air conditioning is standard equipment on F40 to keep cockpit temperature

bearable – windscreen creates a greenhouse effect and side windows provide little ventilation.

black satin finish to the three spokes, is made by Momo; the horn push is a traditional Prancing Horse disc in the centre of the wheel.

The fascia itself is a flat panel running across the width of the car and bending forwards to meet the base of the windscreen. This, too, is so minimal that it flexes to the touch. Creature comforts are absent: there is no clock, and where a glovebox might usually be found there is a rectangular cover (secured by four screws) concealing the fuses and electro-magnetic switches on the electrical panel.

Three air-conditioning vents are positioned below the centre of the fascia and look almost like an afterthought. Two knobs above these vents

Above: Have you ever seen a speedometer reading to 360? It's in kph, of course, but even so this equates to 225mph. Instrument panel is simple, the white calibration

of the dials a model of clarity. Speedo and rev counter are flanked by water temperature and boost gauges. The steering wheel comes from Momo.

control fan speed and temperature. For Ferrari to have fitted air conditioning to a car which is pared to the bone as far as equipment is concerned seems an anomaly, but in fact a source of cool air is essential since the F40's interior would otherwise become unbearably hot on a sunny day. A steady temperature anywhere between 18°C and 32°C can be maintained by adjusting the right-hand control knob.

AIR-CONDITIONING SYSTEM

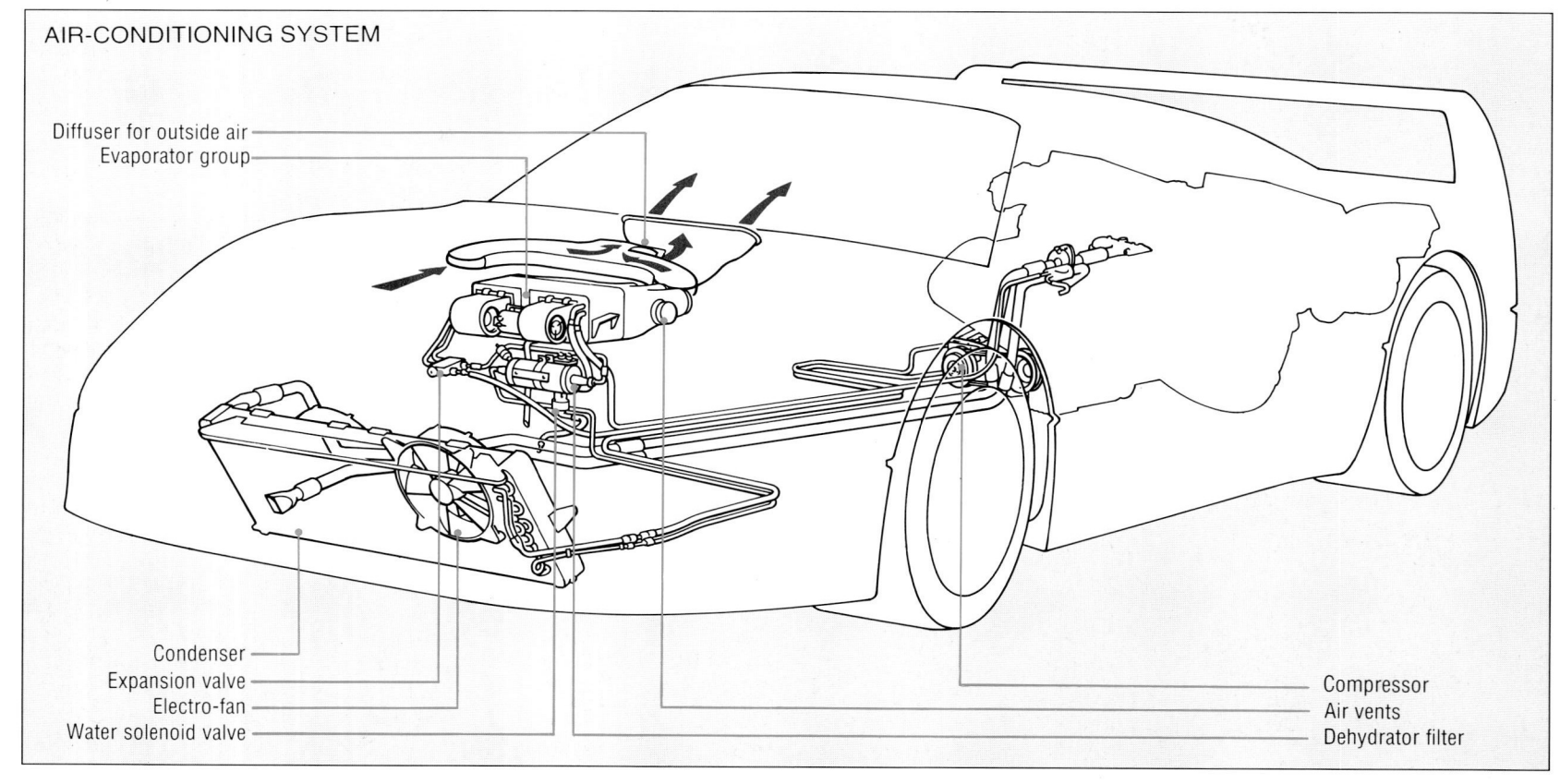

Diffuser for outside air
Evaporator group

Condenser
Expansion valve
Electro-fan
Water solenoid valve

Compressor
Air vents
Dehydrator filter

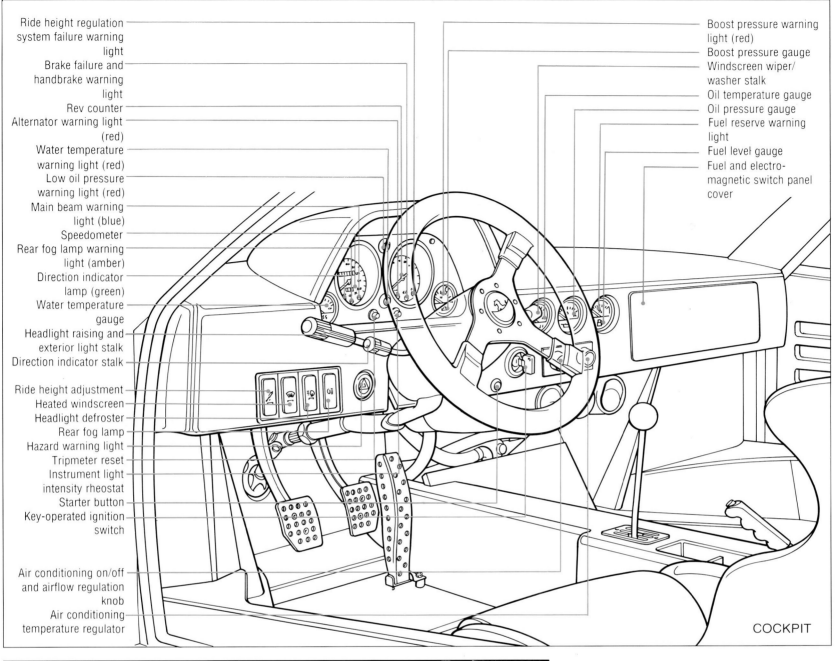

Ride height regulation system failure warning light

Brake failure and handbrake warning light

Rev counter

Alternator warning light (red)

Water temperature warning light (red)

Low oil pressure warning light (red)

Main beam warning light (blue)

Speedometer

Rear fog lamp warning light (amber)

Direction indicator lamp (green)

Water temperature gauge

Headlight raising and exterior light stalk

Direction indicator stalk

Ride height adjustment

Heated windscreen

Headlight defroster

Rear fog lamp

Hazard warning light

Tripmeter reset

Instrument light intensity rheostat

Starter button

Key-operated ignition switch

Air conditioning on/off and airflow regulation knob

Air conditioning temperature regulator

Boost pressure warning light (red)

Boost pressure gauge

Windscreen wiper/ washer stalk

Oil temperature gauge

Oil pressure gauge

Fuel reserve warning light

Fuel level gauge

Fuel and electro-magnetic switch panel cover

COCKPIT

Above: *Diagram of cockpit equipment. The quest for lightness means that only the bare essentials are fitted – there is no radio, nor even a* clock. **Left:** *The pedals are even drilled to save weight – long organ-pedal throttle is ideally positioned for heel and toe operation.*

INSTRUMENTATION
Not quite so minimal

All the instruments are laid out traditionally, with the most important sources of information clustered in a binnacle rising above the upper surface of the fascia and visible through the steering wheel. The two largest dials are the Veglia-Borletti speedometer (left) and electronic rev counter (right), both with conventional – and clear to read – white calibrations on a black background. The speedometer reads to 360kph with markings at 10kph intervals and incorporates a six-figure distance recorder and trip, while the rev counter is marked to 10,000rpm at 250rpm intervals, with the red line at 7500rpm. Metric instruments are fitted for all markets.

Two smaller dials sit either side of these main instruments, the one on the left covering water temperature and that on the right boost pressure (with an inset LED light to indicate a dangerous level of boost). Two warning lights for low oil pressure and high water temperature are placed prominently between the speedometer and rev counter, while below these are two knobs to reset

the trip recorder and to adjust the intensity of the instrument lighting. Further warning lights are found in the bottom sectors of the two main dials; those in the speedometer cover direction indicators, rear fog lights and main beam head lights, while those in the rev counter warn of alternator failure, handbrake on/brake failure and ride height regulation system failure.

Three other gauges are sited in a row, and angled slightly towards the driver, in the centre of the fascia. These cover (from the left) oil temperature, oil pressure and fuel level; a reserve warning light is inset in the fuel gauge. Over on the left-hand side of the fascia are four rocker switches to operate the ride height regulation system, the heated windscreen, the headlight defrosting elements and the rear fog lights; alongside these is a large round button for the hazard warning lights.

The only remaining controls on the fascia are the key-operated ignition switch (and steering lock) and a separate rubber-covered starter button – a racing car traditionally has an individual starter button.

The three column stalks cover the conventional functions. The shorter of the two on the left operates the direction indicators. The longer one has a three-stage movement to operate the exterior lights; pilot lights come on with one twist, a flick downwards brings up the head light pods and switches on dipped beam, and a further movement downwards engages main beam; pulling the lever forwards operates the daytime flashing lights. The right-hand stalk controls the windscreen wipers and washers. Moving it one notch upwards puts the wipers into intermittent mode; another notch gives continuous wiping; a twist gives high-speed operating, and pulling the lever forwards activates the washers.

UNDER THE NOSE
Having to travel light

What little luggage space there is in the F40 is contained under the nose section in a well which was clearly designed to accommodate a spare wheel. Since no spare wheel, not even a 'space-saver', is supplied with the car, this circular cavity can at least take a few small bags. Alternatively, F40 customers can splash out on the three pieces of leather custom luggage made by Mauro Schedoni of Modena.

A comprehensive kit of tools and spare parts is also stowed in this compartment. The tools are a spark plug spanner and ratchet wrench, a set of six spanners, two Philips screwdrivers, two screwdrivers for slotted screws, pliers and a wheel nut spanner. The components include ten spark plugs, a water pump/alternator drive belt, an air-conditioning compressor drive belt, a box of spare bulbs and four pins for the wheel nuts. An Agip puncture repair cylinder and a tyre pressure gauge are also supplied. If towing is necessary, the tow rope has to be attached to an eye bolt which is threaded through a hole in the front spoiler.

Left: Quintessential Ferrari – near-straight gear lever shaft, familiar stainless steel slotted gate at its base, black knob inscribed in white with shift pattern. Five-speed gearbox is heavy to use, requiring a strong pull or push from the shoulder to make a change.

Above: Special luggage is available to prove that you can carry more than a toothbrush in an F40. Made by Mauro Schedoni of Modena, these three pieces – holdall, attaché case, suit slipcase – fit under the nose in a circular well originally designed for a spare wheel.

RACING THE F40
Ferrari F40 Le Mans

Since the Ferrari F40's launch in July 1987, the official word from Maranello has always been that cars would be raced in a quasi-works programme. As this is written, two years later, the F40 Le Mans – as the racing version is to be called – has yet to appear on a starting grid, but at least there is evidence to prove that the car exists.

Although devised by factory people, the racer's development programme has been entrusted to Giuliano Michelotto, the proprietor of a company in Padua which has made a speciality out of developing racing versions of production Ferraris. The plan is that cars should be raced under the wing of Ferrari's foreign importers – a familiar strategy in the past – while enjoying considerable factory assistance. The first such project so far revealed is one organised through Charles Pozzi, the French importer.

High calibre people are working for the Pozzi team. The whole outfit is being masterminded by Jean Sage, Renault's team manager when the company was in Formula One, and among the drivers said to be associated with the project are Patrick Tambay (one-time Ferrari Formula One driver), Jean-Pierre Jabouille (for four seasons a Renault Formula One driver) and Jacques Lafitte (winner of six Grands Prix for Ligier). It is likely that the team will also have sponsorship from Marlboro when it eventually races.

Since the F40 evolved from a racing design, the GTO Evoluzione, relatively little modification has been necessary. On the engine front, larger IHI turbochargers and intercoolers are used to increase boost to 2.1bar, together with 'hotter' camshafts and a modified Weber-Marelli electronic engine management system. As a result, power output rises from the standard 478bhp to at least 750bhp, a figure which is more than competitive against Sports-Prototype World Championship contenders. The five-speed gearbox is strengthened and a tougher Borg & Beck clutch is used.

The suspension is fundamentally the same, but the geometry has been altered to suit the characteristics of racing tyres. The brakes are uprated to match the extra power. Although chassis stiffness is already of a high order on the production F40, changes have been made to offset its weight disadvantage compared with the race-bred aluminium and composite monocoques of modern endurance sports racers. The F40's carbonfibre/Kevlar stiffening panels have been extended and parts of its steel lattice frame altered to create a lighter structure – but the manner of construction remains the same. It is believed that weight has been reduced from the production 2425lb (1100kg) to around 2315lb (1050kg); the F40 started off with such a light structure that opportunities for further reductions have been few.

The F40's aerodynamics have had to be tuned to handle a top speed in the region of 220mph; in the interests of front downforce, a flexible extension has been added to the nose spoiler and angled strakes run back to the front wheelarches. A new outlet from the front water radiator is set into the bonnet between the headlight pods. The rear wing has a central aluminium support to prevent flexing above 200mph, and an extra lip has been attached to the trailing edge of the aerofoil; further aluminium plates are used to create channels to keep airflow tidy as it leaves the car's underside.

The team's original plan at the outset of 1989 had been to take part in the GTC category of the Sports-Prototype World Championship, with the Le Mans 24 Hours as its main goal. As the world's most important endurance race, Le Mans is an obvious ambition for Ferrari's sports car racing comeback. Ferrari has not won the French classic since 1965, when Jochen Rindt and Masten Gregory scored the last of six consecutive victories at the circuit. As the season unfolded, however, the cars failed to appear in World Championship events, the team stating that it would instead take part in the German Super Cup (a series of sprint races for endurance cars) in order to develop the cars in readiness for a full season in 1990. However, it seemed unlikely that any racing F40s will have been seen in public by the end of 1989.

As well as intensive testing at Fiorano, the car has been evaluated at Monza (the home of the Italian Grand Prix) by Dario Benuzzi and Jean-Pierre Jabouille. This circuit allows much higher speeds than Fiorano, and it is believed that suspect engine reliability – broken turbos in particular – at sustained speed is the chief reason for the programme's delay. Of course, this is a crucial flaw as far as Le Mans is concerned: having an engine able to cope with the three-mile Mulsanne Straight is a prerequisite for success at the French circuit.

The word is that in 1990 F40s will be raced in the Sports-Prototype World Championship and the IMSA Championship in the USA, and that US importer Luigi Chinetti may join Charles Pozzi with a North American Racing Team (NART) entry at Le Mans. Ferrari's plans may have got off to a false start, but the will is there to recapture those former days of Maranello glory in endurance racing.

Below: Changes to improve the F40's aerodynamics on this 1989 racing prototype include a flexible extension to the noise spoiler, angled strakes at either side of the nose and a new radiator air outlet on the bonnet.

MANUFACTURE

Composite materials require new techniques — how Ferrari builds the limited-run F40

F40s FORM SUCH a small proportion of Ferrari's output – between 5 and 10 per cent – that the short production line squeezed between the rows for V8, V12 and flat-12 cars occupies a tiny area of the Maranello factory. Here a hand-picked group of Ferrari's 1750-strong workforce build the cars at a noticeably more relaxed pace than their colleagues around them to produce finished F40s at a rate of one or two per day. They are all meticulous, skilled people who have had to learn many new techniques to build a car which differs strongly from mainstream Ferrari production. Their plum jobs seem to given them an air of contentment as they go about their work.

F40 ASSEMBLY
Building with pride

The F40 manufacturing arrangement is the familiar one of stations on a mass-production track, but at Maranello partially completed cars move down the line when they are ready, not according to a tight schedule which would encourage slapdash work. Each worker is also assigned a vast range of tasks, the theory being that job satisfaction is high and quality consistently good. It seems to work, because Ferrari quality today is higher than it has ever been. In the case of the F40, the final assembly line starts with the arrival of chassis units to which mechanical sub-structures are fitted in stages, and finishes with complete cars which can be driven away under their own power.

A good proportion of an F40's construction does not take place at Maranello. Chassis units are assembled at the Scaglietti body-manufacturing plant in Modena, where all Ferrari's (except the Testarossa and 412s built at Pininfarina) start life before making the 10-mile trip by transporter to Maranello. The composite parts arrive at Scaglietti from three suppliers – TIR of Parma, Holding System of Rome and Enichem of Milan – and the tubular steel chassis from Vaccara of Modena. When the time inevitably comes for composite structural materials to be used more widely in Ferrari production, it is likely that investment will be made in the expertise and autoclave equipment necessary to produce them in-house; the technology is familiar to Racing

Below: All composite body panels are made up before they are fitted to the car; here a pair of doors receive a seal of mastic between bodywork and plexiglass window. Bottom: Each hollow door and window structure weighs no more than 3.3lb (1.5kg).

Department people, but their facilities are geared to producing a handful of Formula One cars, not parts in their hundreds. For the moment Ferrari finds it more convenient to rely on outside suppliers to cope with the problems of manufacturing these components, dealing itself only with their assembly.

Body pieces in composite are also made by these suppliers and assembled by Ferrari. The rate of production is limited by the fact that working with these materials is so time-consuming – an F40 tail section, complete with wing uprights and slatted back window, takes three days to make. In the early days of production, through the second half of 1988, F40 output was as low as half a car per day (although the target was two per day) because composite body panels were taking longer than expected to make. By the end of 1988 only forty-eight F40s had been delivered – at that rate it would take ten years to build a run of close to 1000! Things quickened up in 1989, helped by the pressure of having to deliver cars to most European markets before the stricter safety and engine emissions laws introduced at the end of the year.

After careful finishing to make sure that the composite weave of external body surfaces is as flat as possible, Glasurit acrylic paint – always in that vivid Ferrari red described as Rosso Corsa – is sprayed on to the twelve individual pieces by hand at Marenello, and topped by a lacquer layer. Finished body panels arrive at the production line on a jig ready to be attached to the car. Some finishing work is required on the line: for example, fitting up the aerofoil part of the rear wing structure and applying mastic to seal joins between body and plexiglass windows.

Above: Each F40 chassis arrives at the start of the Maranello assembly line in this state, with some cockpit bodywork and the rear under-valance in place. Stout extension frame for supporting engine, gearbox and rear suspension can be seen clearly.

Below: Supported on a jig, an embryonic F40 begins its journey down the line. The front part of the chassis provides attachment points for front suspension and steering, none of which has been fitted at this early stage – water radiator and fans are already in place.

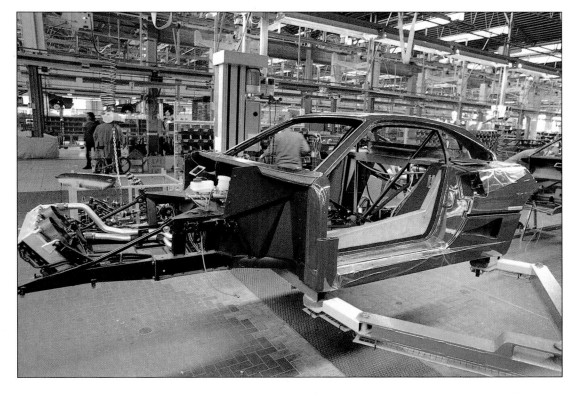

STATIONS ON THE WAY
Starting with basics

There are only five stations on the F40 line, so part-finished cars roll forward to the next stage only once or twice a day. The first two stages are concerned with the fitment of basic ancillaries to the bare chassis/body shells – only cockpit bodywork and the rear under-valance are attached to the chassis when a car arrives at the line. Titanium-based heat-resistant skins go into the engine bay before the gearbox and engine oil coolers, some of the pipework and the pair of fuel tanks. Rear suspension (including the brakes) and driveshafts are added at the same time. The bare interior slowly takes shape with the installation of the gear linkage, handbrake, pedals, steering column, Bosch relay/fuse panel and metal seat runners. The water radiator and its electric fans, battery, air conditioning, braking system and steering rack are fitted to the front of the car.

The third stage sees the engine and gearbox — a complete assembly constructed in another part of the factory — lowered into the car to attach to mounting points on the chassis extensions behind the cabin. Once everything is aligned and bolted home, all the pipework and electrical systems are connected up, and the final part of the exhaust system — transverse silencer box and three outlet pipes — is installed. By the time the front suspension and brakes are fitted, the car is close to mechanical completion.

Some of the minimal interior equipment goes in at the fourth stage. All the trim pieces are sections of moulded glassfibre or aluminium sheet covered with felt, or, in the case of the headlining, plastic. The instrument pack, switchgear, composite seat shells, steering wheel and safety belts are fitted to bring the cabin close to its finished state. Wheels and tyres are also attached, and installing the big carbonfibre/Kevlar circular luggage well completes the assembly process at the front. The remaining sections of bodywork — doors, nose and tail — are fitted at the last stage before a final check on suspension geometry and electrical systems. There is a dramatic visual transformation when the large sections of body-work are attached, for a car which looks a long way from completion suddenly becomes a real F40 in just half an hour.

Many of the components fitted to the F40 come from outside suppliers: radiators from AKG and Setrab, electric fans from Spal, steering rack from TRW Italia, instruments from Veglia-Borletti, safety belts from Sabelt, brakes from Brembo,

shock absorbers from Koni, turbochargers from IHI, intercoolers from Behr, most electrical items from Bosch, the ignition-injection system from Weber-Marelli and wheels from Speedline. Like all Ferrari's other models, however, the F40's engine and gearbox is made largely in-house.

CASTING ENGINE AND GEARBOX
Hot metal at Maranello

The process begins in Maranello's foundry, sited near the main gate in one of the oldest parts of the factory complex. Cylinder blocks, heads and gear-box castings are cast in an alloy which comprises 90 per cent aluminium, 9.4 per cent silicon and 0.6 per cent of other metals (including magnesium, iron, copper, manganese and titanium). These parts are traditionally sand-cast in mould-ing boxes. The boxes are used repeatedly, but

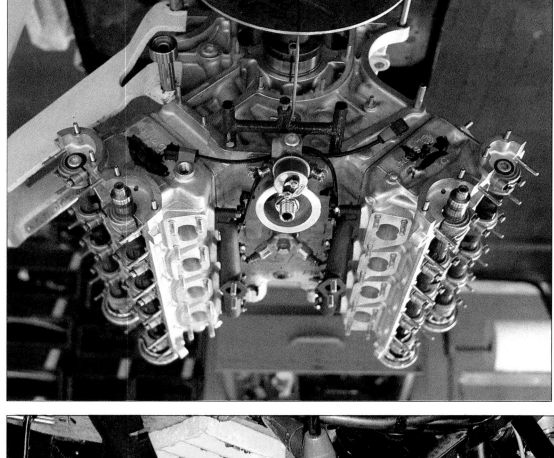

Above: One of three stations in the tiny engine assembly area at Maranello. V8's classic 90° angle can be seen at this point, where cylinder heads have just been fitted. The camshafts remain exposed until those famous crackle-finish red cam covers go on.

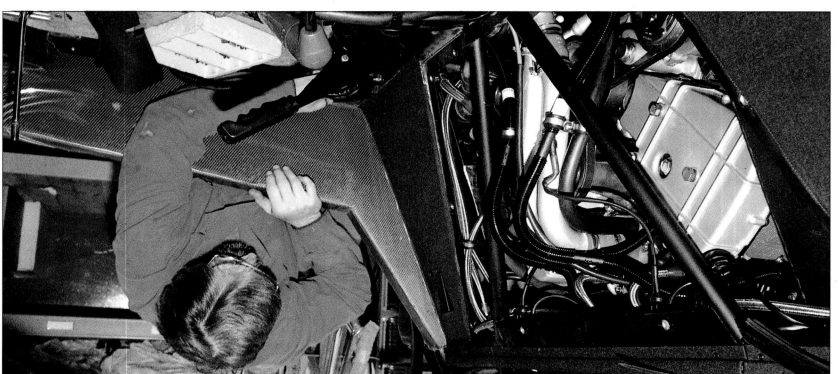

Above: When engine is in place it sits close to passenger compartment rear bulkhead to optimise front/rear weight distribution. Detachable bulkhead panel helps in the assembly process, and also, importantly, improves accessibility for servicing.

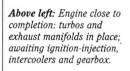

Above left: *Engine close to completion: turbos and exhaust manifolds in place; awaiting ignition-injection, intercoolers and gearbox.*

Above right: *Tunnel through centre of cabin takes gear linkage, handbrake cable and cooling system hoses from radiator.*

Below left: *Early stage in interior assembly: fascia, air conditioning outlets, wiring looms and steering column are fitted.*

Below right: *Basic interior trim is fitted once most of mechanical assembly is completed; here fascia has received its grey felt covering.*

Bottom left: *Rear under-valance provides a home for Setrab gearbox oil cooler (engine oil cooler is on opposite side).*

Bottom right: *AKG water radiator is cooled by two Spal electric fans; note aluminium pipes running back from radiator to engine.*

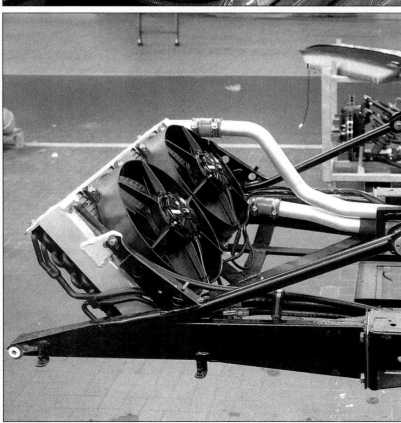

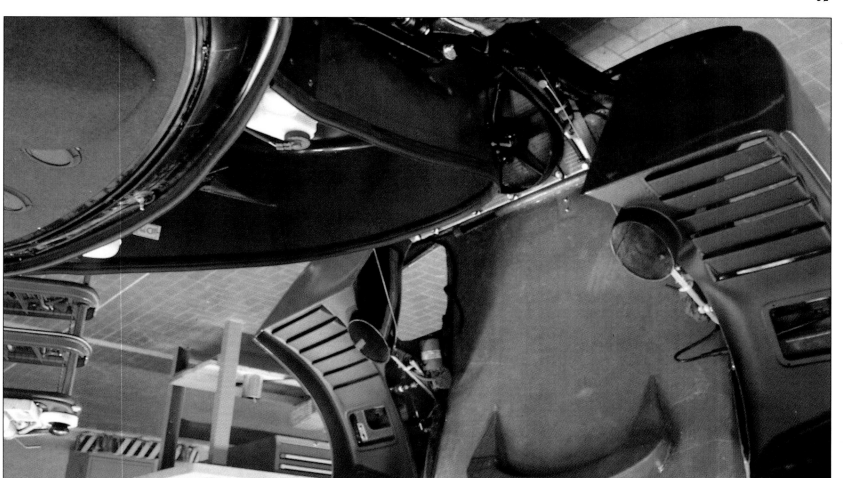

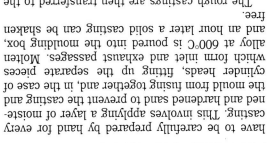

Above: Rear suspension has classic double wishbone layout and Koni shock absorbers enclosed by co-axial coil springs. Note drilled and ventilated discs carry secondary calipers on trailing edge for handbrake.

Below: Windscreen has yet to be fitted but car now stands on its wheels. Front-hinged nose section is an elaborate structure – circular ducts to front brakes and two-into-one air-conditioning intake can be seen.

SUPERCARS: FERRARI F40

have to be carefully prepared by hand for every casting. This involves applying a layer of moiste-ned and hardened sand to prevent the casting and the mould from fusing together and, in the case of cylinder heads, fitting up the separate pieces which form inlet and exhaust passages. Molten alloy at 600°C is poured into the moulding box, and an hour later a solid casting can be shaken free.

The rough castings are then transferred to the main part of the factory to be machined automati-cally, alongside the engine parts for the other model ranges, on the computerised Mandelli equipment which makes up Ferrari's Flexible Manufacturing System (FMS). Craftsmanship plays a large role in the F40's manufacture, but here the human touch is eliminated. These preci-sion robots carry out all drilling and machining, depositing finished pieces which are ready for the painstaking business of assembly. To see such sophisticated automation invariably surprises people visiting Maranello for the first time, espe-cially as the size of the FMS area looks quite vast for a company producing only 4000 cars annually. Fiat's investment in modernising Ferrari's produc-tion facilities in the early 1980s made it possible. Only three engine/gearbox assemblies can be built up at a time in the tiny area reserved for the twin-turbo V8. One of the handful of skilled technicians working here starts with a bare cylin-der block into which liners, main bearings and crankshaft (machined from the solid) are inserted. Cylinder heads, each with a pair of hardened steel camshafts and sixteen valves, are assembled separately before being mounted to the block. Red crackle finish cam covers are added before the gearbox and clutch bell housing are joined. The final stages are to fit the ignition-injection compo-nents and manifolding to the top of the engine, mate up the two turbocharging installations and fit ancillaries such as the starter motor and alternator.

Above: Completed F40s move under their own power for the first time when they reach the end of the line.

Only detail finishing – this car has yet to receive day-time flashing lights and glass fairings – remains.

Below: After 125 miles (200km) of testing on public roads and at Fiorano, F40s return to the finishing shop

for pre-sale preparation. Any comments from test drivers are dealt with; paint chips may need attention.

TESTING TIMES
Bench, road and track

Complete engines are taken to the engine test cell area for at least four hours of bench running. After a period of slow running to bed down all the components, the engine is tested at a range of higher speeds to check power and torque output, oil pressure, water temperature, fuel consumption and emissions levels. Only when it has been signed off can an engine join the stock alongside the main assembly line, ready for installation in a car.

Like all other Ferrari models, every F40 is road-tested upon completion around the Fiorano test track and for 125 miles (200km) over public roads. Only when this evaluation has been completed – and any problems dealt with – is a car taken to the finishing shop for thorough cleaning and final preparation prior to sale. Every Ferrari goes through this spotless place where dirt is banished by vibrating door mats, air conditioning and scrupulous spring cleaning. Further fault rectification may be necessary at this stage, although generally the work is confined to touching up paint blemishes and stone chips incurred on the road test, fitting out the car with details like handbook, labels and tools, and applying protective coverings to bodywork and interior for the journey to the customer.

At last a finished F40 is ready to be delivered, or in some cases picked up direct from the factory by the customer. So great has been the interest in the car – and the certainty of its instant investment potential – that the entire production run, whatever it turns out be, was pre-sold soon after launch. A customer may have waited several years before he finally gets his hands on his car.

Explosive in performance, the F40 towers above all other supercars; yet there is a docile side to its nature too

DRIVING THE F40

Below: The F40 has such hard-tuned suspension that body roll is almost non-existent, although the g-force being generated here – on the steering pad at Fiorano – exceeds any other road car; test driver Fiorenzo Fornari likens the grip to that of a Group C2 sports racer.

MONG THE KALEIDOSCOPE of sensations which tumbled through my head after a day out on the road with a Ferrari F40, one moment stuck in my mind the most vividly. In just a few seconds on a motorway slip-road, the F40 revealed for the first time its quite extraordinary acceleration. In second gear and with my right foot thrust to the floor, here at last, after many miles of suburban dawdling, was a brief chance to take the engine above 3000rpm and give the F40 its head. A moment to tighten my grip on the steering wheel, to sharpen my concentration, to prepare myself for a burst of energy from the world's fastest road car.

I have never experienced such awe-inspiring force on four wheels. All had been calm when driving slowly, and then, like a bullet from a gun, the F40 simply exploded up the road, its exhaust note strengthening into a guttural roar, rear tyres chewing into the tarmac. In an instant it climbed from the pace of a man's run to match the speed of traffic passing on the motorway, leaving the photographer's Golf GTI as a distant speck in its wake. That mighty push through to 7500rpm occurred so quickly that I had both hands on the steering wheel only for a split second before it was time to reach for third gear, ease off the throttle and blend into the flow. In one surge of second gear acceleration the F40 had made its statement; and it could do exactly the same again in three more gears.

A

Leaving the rest behind

There are many supercars which set the pulse racing with their towering performance, but no Countach, Testarossa, 911 Turbo, Daytona or Bora will ever feel quite the same again. They are merely quick; the F40 is blisteringly fast. So unbelievably fast that you need space, a completely empty stretch of road, even to think about flexing the right foot. In moments of armchair reverie I had wondered what the F40's slingshot acceleration might feel like, yet the reality was more explosive than I could have imagined possible in a road car. How can those massive rear tyres, close in size to Formula One rubber, possibly claw such power to the road? How can drive shafts take such brute force without twisting like toffee?

This F40 day out, the pinnacle of my driving experience which I shall cherish forever, began in Egham, Surrey, at Maranello Concessionaires Ltd, Britain's Ferrari importer. It was a perfect summer morning when I arrived to find the car sparkling in the sun on the showroom forecourt, spitting a muffled burble from its exhaust as it idled gently. Owned by the company, this F40 is one of only three in Britain at the time of writing, and the first to have been imported. Managing Director Roger Maingot was the lucky man who drove it back from Italy in July 1988. Like the other fifty or so F40s destined for British customers, no changes have been made to suit the right-hand drive market; the steering wheel is on the left and the speedometer is calibrated in kilometres per hour.

There is time to stroll round the car, taking in

F40 ET AL.

this waist-high beast which intimidates by its very presence. It is too overtly aggressive in shape to be considered truly beautiful, but it looks terrific from all angles. From the front the great width of the flattened bonnet dominates the appearance, while the imposing wing and sharply cut-off bodywork emphasise the purposeful look from the rear. To my eyes the F40 looks best from the side, with all the raked angles of bodywork, windscreen and ducting telling you that this car can travel fast. All it needs to be at home on a Le Mans starting grid is a set of white roundels and racing numbers.

Through the matt black tail grille and plexiglass back window can be seen the engine, gearbox and suspension, laid out like any Group C sports racing car. Looking along planes of body-

Below: Nothing about the F40's appearance is understated. The deep nose spoiler, vast rear wing, low-slung build and plexiglass sliding side windows add up to a picture of competition

breeding. All it needs to be at home on a Le Mans starting grid is a set of white roundels and racing numbers – indeed, Ferrari's plan is that F40s can be raced with relatively little modification.

Above: Despite 335/35 ZR 17 tyres at the back (the widest rubber ever seen on a road car), the rear wheels can be provoked out of line at will. Driven hard, the F40

slides through corners with precision, dramatic angles of oversteer its natural way – but driving with such abandon must be saved for the race circuit.

work against the light reveals the faint weave pattern of composite fabric under layers of Rosso Corsa paint (you can have your F40 any colour you like as long as it's red). The plexiglass sliding side windows are a distractingly crude detail laid onto this functional shape, but they add to the F40's visual message of competition breeding.

I am handed a set of keys which look innocuous enough to belong to any workaday car. There is a large one for ignition with a discreet Prancing Horse embossed in the rubber grip, and two little ones – fiddly things which look like keys to a cheap padlock – to cover locks on the doors, fuel filler, engine cover and front lid. When someone has not already kindly fired up the car for you, an F40 is started by turning the key through 180° for ignition and then pressing a separate rubber starter button.

FIRST IMPRESSIONS
Making myself at home

Lifting a small, flush lever below the side window opens the driver's door, which is such a featherlight structure of composite and plexiglass that a gentle breeze pushes it around like a piece of paper. It seems brutal to slam the door shut once you have folded yourself down into the seat, but it needs a good tug to latch securely, with a plasticky rattle. The driving seat, like the passenger one a simple composite shell upholstered with thin padding and scarlet velour, is set low on the floor, so that you sit with legs straight ahead feeling very close to the road.

The seat is adjustable only in a fore/aft direction by means of a bar underneath your legs, but its relatively upright position is very comfortable, pronounced scallops at your shoulders and hips hugging your body tightly. Apparently a customer who collects his F40 from the factory is given a choice of three seat sizes so that he can select the best fit. This F40 has conventional inertia reel safety belts which are easy to wear, but anchorage points (and slots in the seat backs) are supplied

SUPERCARS: FERRARI F40

for fitting a racing-type four-point harness. Just the job to hold you in place during hard driving, but a nuisance if you are hopping in and out of the car on a shopping trip.

Only the height of the non-adjustable Momo steering wheel mars the driving position, for my build at least. I found the wheel several inches too high when held at the quarter-to-three position with thumbs tucked round the horizontal spokes, so that I felt as if I had to adopt a slightly sit-up-and-beg position. Otherwise it is a delicious tiller to grip, of just the right size and with a pleasantly chunky rim bound with black leather. The horn push, of course, is a traditional central button bearing the Prancing Horse motif. The pedals, elegant plates of drilled and shaped aluminium, are positioned to perfection; the spacing between them is just right, while the organ-pedal throttle which extends down to the floor is ideally aligned for comfortable heel and toe operation. A clutch foot rest, moulded as a protrusion from the composite floor, is a neat and thoughtful touch.

INTO THE COCKPIT
A study in minimalism

To say that the cockpit is spartan is an under-statement – there is more trim in a no-frills Yugo. The only soft furnishings inside the F40 are the splash of colour on the seats, some expanses of simple graphite grey felt (across the fascia to prevent windscreen reflections, along the gear linkage tunnel, up the windscreen pillars and over the rear bulkhead) and dove grey headlining in perforated plastic. Everywhere else in the cabin the F40 displays its competition-inspired structure in the raw.

Charcoal grey carbonfibre panels lightened by yellow strands of Kevlar make up the bare floor and footwells, their surfaces scuffed by feet. Two rectangular girders form deep sill sections which run either side of the cabin, emphasising the feeling that you sit low in the car. The joints between composite panels are bonded with bright green adhesive, applied a little unevenly like plastic weld lines. Even the doors are hollow, the exposed inner surface of the body appearing brownish-yellow owing to the predominance of Kevlar in the weave; conveniently, the bare door cavities actually provide generous stowage space. You release the doors from the inside by tugging a plastic-covered cable hanging down into the hollow like a length of clothes-line, just like an old Mini. Come to think of it, sliding side windows are reminiscent of an early Mini too.

Instrumentation and switchgear is similarly minimal; all the essential dials and controls can be found on the simple fascia, but no superfluous ones. The important information is contained in a small binnacle positioned so that no dials or warning lights are masked by the steering wheel rim. Veglia-Borletti gauges with simple white calibration on a black background are a welcome change from Ferrari's usual – and less clear – orange-on-black style. The two large dials, of course, are a speedometer (reading to 360kph) and a rev counter (to 10,000rpm, red-lined at 7750rpm), while either side of them are little gauges for water temperature on the left and boost pressure on the right. Three more instruments covering (from left to right) oil temperature, oil pressure and fuel level are sited in a row

Right: F40 owned by Maranello Concessionaires Ltd was first to be imported into Britain, in mid-1988. Pleasing angle shows F40's beauty and purpose to best effect, but what a shame that British registration plate – does any country have larger plates? – looks so bald.

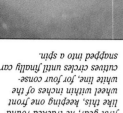

along the centre of the fascia and angled towards the driver.

Since the F40 has absolutely no unnecessary gadgetry, finding the rest of the controls does not take long; all you discover are the devices a car needs to function. Forget all the modern gizmos — electric windows, powered sunroof, electric door mirrors with heating elements, central locking — with which any self-respecting executive car is now loaded. The F40 does not even have a clock. Only two items of its equipment, the air condition-ing and heated windscreen, could conceivably be regarded as inessential. Not so. The greenhouse effect of that large windscreen makes air condi-tioning indispensable to keep cockpit temperature bearable on a hot day, while the absence of a conventional heater means that heating elements are the only way to demist the windscreen on a cold morning or during rain.

Three column stalks from the Fiat parts bin, two on the left and one on the right, look after the conventional functions. The longer left-hand lever operates the lights, the shorter one the indicators; windscreen wipers and washers are operated by the right-hand lever. Two simple knobs in the centre of the fascia control air-conditioning fan speed and temperature, while the hazard warning lights are operated by a push button to the left of the steering column. All that remains, next to the driver's door, is a row of Fiat switches controlling front fog lamps, high-intensity rear lamps and windscreen heater. A slot for a fourth switch in this row is blank; the F40 handbook assigns it to the optional ride height control which has yet to find its way into production.

ONTO THE ROAD
Learning how the F40 feels

My aim is to find out what the F40 is like to live with for a day of normal driving, how this king among supercars feels to hustle along favourite minor roads, to travel on motorways, even to crawl along congested urban roads.

My fears that it will be difficult to handle in traffic turn out to be largely unfounded, for the F40 is surprisingly usable at speeds up to a sixth of its maximum. It is not as easy to drive on first acquaintance as a Testarossa or 328GTB, but it is far from intimidating. Initial acclimatisation is a case of getting used to the weight of its controls and its relative lack of visibility.

The F40 demands a notably robust approach from its driver, although all modern Ferraris are generally heavier to handle than run-of-the-mill modern tin boxes. The controls all operate beauti-fully — they just require effort from certain muscles never taxed by more mundane machin-ery. The clutch needs a stout push to the floor, so much so that it feels inordinately heavy until you adapt to it. Considering the prodigious power it has to transmit, however, it works with a delight-fully progressive action, easing so sweetly through its biting point that you can pull away happily from rest without so much as a tickle on the accelerator pedal. This is a surprise — I had

expected the odd stall along the way. The brakes, too, require a fair degree of leg-work to begin to produce good stopping power, particularly when they are cold. So great is the F40's performance that the brakes are designed to work best when they are cold. As a result there is some heat in discs and pads when they need a firm stamp in gentler driving, during which slowing down is accompanied by a metallic squeal generated by hard pads working below optimum temperature. The accelerator pedal also offers more than average resistance, although having to apply some pressure to it in no way detracts from its silky action. Tempting though it is to squeeze on the loud pedal at any opportunity, it is perfectly easy to trickle along on the most slender of throttle openings.

F40 GEARBOX
Quintessential Ferrari

Just as the pedals have the weighty feel of a competition car, the gearbox also has a meaty quality. In time-honoured Ferrari fashion, the lever is straightforwardly functional, not the kind of stylised plastic sculpture which passes for a gearchange in most modern cars. A vertical shaft of steel pokes through a slotted gate and is crowned by a shiny black knob the size of a golf ball. Simple, traditional and quintessentially Fer-rari. Of all the special sensations which come with

Above: Another handling shot at Fiorano, Ferrari's figure-of-eight test track. In back to back comparisons with a Porsche 959 (the only other supercar in the F40's performance league), test driver Dario Benuzzi found the Italian car to be 10sec a lap quicker than the German rival — it was 20mph faster down the straight.

Below: Test driver Forman demonstrates the F40's progressive oversteering nature while hammering round the Fiorano steering pad. Using all 478bhp in first gear, he tracked round like this, keeping one front wheel within inches of the white line, for four conse-cutive circles until finally snapped into a spin.

driving a Maranello machine, none is quite as evocative as the chunk-chunk of metal meeting metal as you manhandle the gearchange from slot to slot. Shuffling the cogs is not a matter of flicking the wrist in the F40: the lever needs a firm shove from the shoulder and deliberate cross-wise movement across the gate. The pattern of the five forward speeds starts with a dog-leg first towards you and back, with second/third in the next plane and fourth/fifth away from you. Engaging reverse, which is opposite first, requires a strong push downwards on the lever before the gear will slip home. Selecting first and second gears is hard work when the gearbox oil is cold, but fine when everything has warmed through.

Apart from developing a sense of the weight of all these controls so that you can start to use them confidently, the other aspect of the F40

which takes some getting used to is the restricted visibility from the driver's seat. Seeing to the front and sides is fine, but the lack of a good rearward view is a problem when looking for gaps in traffic. The interior mirror's field of vision is fine, but the translucent quality of the plexiglass back window means that a clear view is available only through its cooling slots. Since these slots are arranged in two rows, the central rib of plexiglass partially obscures cars sitting directly behind, turning them into fuzzy blobs rather than crisp images. It sounds an inane criticism of a car in which you might expect rearward vision to be some way down the list of priorities, but I found this lack of a good view behind a distinct handicap when handling the F40 in traffic.

Considering the immense breadth of the F40's haunches (overall width is only 0.2in. (5mm) less

Above: F40 looks breathtaking from this rear three-quarter angle. Notice the air outlet behind the front wheel (mud thrown up by the wheels coats the doors in wet weather!), tiny door handle, fuel filler cover behind it, and lateral slots under the wing for engine cooling.

than a Testarossa, which itself is the widest car in production), visibility from the two door mirrors is excellent. They give a sharp image, with no vibration, although the field of view is quite narrow. Turning round to look through the rear three-quarters of the car at a junction or round-about gives you a view shielded by C-pillar body-work and the passenger seat's high back, but there are other supercars – Countach among them – which present more difficulties in traffic. In wet weather, I am told, the rear three-quarter windows are prone to misting up, although engine heat keeps the back window clear.

EARLY MILEAGE IN THE F40
Remarkably easy in traffic

What is so surprising about the F40 in these early miles, however, is how very obliging it feels when the going is slow. The clutch is far too progressive ever to snatch, throttle movement is sensitive and the unassisted rack and pinion steering is quite light even when the car is barely moving. Coping with the weight of non-servo brakes is the only tough part of treating the F40 as a town car. Above all, the engine is quite remarkably tractable for a unit which punches out four times the power of a good hot hatchback. Once upon a time the inevitable penalty of driving a supercar on congested roads would be the misfiring, spluttering and coughing caused by oiled plugs. The F40 shows no sign of any such complaint, the V8 simply pulling as sweetly and gently at low revs as any lazy American V8. Considering its cataclysmic response higher up the scale, this low-down delicacy is quite uncanny.

I am already warming to the F40's friendliness when I join the motorway and wind up the speed occasionally to around merely half its maximum. As the pace quickens, the car's board-like ride starts to feel rather more composed, levelling out to give more comfortable progress. But the overwhelming impression is of the noise that is generated as the scenery starts to flash by. The bare cockpit seems to act as a sounding box, turning the thump of tyres over cats' eyes into claps of thunder and the slap of rubber across surface ripples into a volley of popping champagne corks. You hear an intense rush of wind whistling around the car overlaid by the rustling of eddies around door mirrors and side windows. All this heightens the sensation of speed, but it makes conversation with a passenger impossible above 90mph (145kph), all but drowning the sound of the engine as well. For a short distance the unrelenting cacophony is bearable, but over a journey of hundreds of miles I can imagine that it could tarnish your relationship with your F40. No wonder that not even a radio is fitted: you would never hear it.

Dynamically, the car feels totally relaxed at these speeds, which are mere child's play for it. With its mellow note trying vainly to pierce the gale of sounds, the engine drifts along at around 3700rpm in fifth gear at 100mph (161kph), the

Above: F40 at speed. It's a noisy car, the spartan cockpit seeming to act as a sounding box. Tyre and wind roar combine to produce so much noise that conversation is difficult above 90mph – one can only imagine how much the cacophony adds to the sensation of speed at 200mph.

turbos just beginning to nudge in a whisker of boost so that a quick whoosh of acceleration can open up space from lesser cars snapping at the car's heels. The F40 tracks in a straight line with absolute precision, the steering jiggling gently in your hands to communicate every surface irregularity. The car is still reined in, but now it is just beginning to show a glimmer of its true potential.

INTO ITS ELEMENT
Finding space for the F40

Once we are off the motorway, the sheer stature of the F40's performance becomes clear. It is so outrageously fast, swinging through corners as well as squirting down straights, that speed-limited public roads are too small for it. You really do need the space and freedom of a race track to explore the highest realms of its performance; the nearest you can get in the public domain is on broad, quiet, well-surfaced minor roads with good open views across the corners, and even then restraint must come before valour. But there were a few sinuous roads across the downlands of southern England where the F40 could reveal further facets of its character, and confirm just how dramatically Ferrari has rewritten the boundaries of supercar performance with this single masterpiece. In particular, one three-mile stretch – an open strip of road without tall hedges, farm entrances and side turnings (the sort that could give any driver pleasure) – was just the place to raise the pace.

The twin-turbo V8 is a quite incredible engine when it climbs on boost at around 3000rpm. What has already been felt as a vivid push from behind up to this point is suddenly intensified into a glorious torrent of power unleashed with all the ferocity of a jet engine's afterburn. The car stabs forward with such a kick that you really do need to tighten your grip on the wheel, glancing alternately from road to rev counter to make sure that you snatch the next gear, right hand off the wheel for not a moment longer than necessary, before that gyrating needle flicks too close to the red sector on the dial. The car squats down, the steering lightens, the engine note hardens, the rear tyres tear at the road for grip. It all but paws the ground in anticipation.

Over anything but the smoothest surface this magnificent thrust challenges the ability of the tyres to cope, each bump creating a momentary loss of traction. The car rockets forward with its staggering force in a series of lunges, the back tyres biting and slipping, biting and slipping. It is all so awesome, the wheelspin so ever-present, that you judge your moment carefully before releasing ultimate throttle-to-the-floor acceleration in second or third gears, even fourth. It is this constant assault on the limits of traction as much as the engine's power which determines how fast the F40 will accelerate.

While the engine's outright muscle so often tests the ability of the chassis to handle it, the manner of its delivery is superb. There is barely a trace of the turbo lag which so often ruins the responsiveness of forced-induction motors, for the engine answers virtually instantaneously to the throttle. It produces a rapid and savage punch, of course, but when you get the measure of it you come to realise that the swelling of boost is beautifully progressive, helping the driver to manage the F40's absurdly spectacular road performance. Far from having a notable top-end bias, the spread of power is so wide that peak torque of 425lb ft is developed at a lowly 4000rpm. Indeed, the arrival of boost is so measured and instant that you tend to forget the presence of twin turbos until the wastegate mutters when you lift off the power.

HANDLING AND BALANCE
Superb cornering ability
Competition-bred machine that it is, the F40's handling character is about as stiff and sporting as you will find in a road car. There is sprung suspension, although at times the car's kart-like behaviour has you doubting it. Much of this sense of stiffness, I feel sure, stems from the rigidity of the chassis, for the whole car has a quite distinct feeling of solidity when cornering hard, as if there really is not a trace of flex in the composite/steel structure. The result is utterly faithful cornering behaviour when the road surface is smooth, choppiness when it is not.

Cornering balance is perfect. On a trailing throttle the nose tends to run wide until it is balanced by feeding in power judiciously, causing the line to sharpen as the rear wheels bite. You have a strong sense that unfettered power could overcome the grip of those rear gumballs, but they stay anchored to their line in the dry when you drive within the margins of sense on public roads; goodness knows how readily they break away on a slippery surface. The sheer speed with which the F40 can attack bends, almost completely without body roll, is bewildering, but withdrawing the power eases the car undramatically onto a tighter line should you find that you have misjudged a turn.

In truth, four laps of Fiorano a few months earlier alongside Ferrari test driver Fiorenzo Fornari had been rather more revealing of the F40's cornering ability. Fornari's relaxed handling of the car on a track he knows intimately had shown just how controllably the F40's oversteer arrives, the tail shifting fluidly sideways under full power. Driven hard, the F40 slides through corners with precision, dramatic angles of oversteer its natural way. Once Fornari pushed too hard: when the rear tyres finally gave up their unequal struggle to harness such power, the car snapped into a spin too rapidly even for the expert to catch it. But this happened at heady speeds, the sort of pace, said Fornari, that would not disgrace a Group C2 sports racer on slick tyres.

So much of the pleasure of powering the F40 into a series of bends, savouring the rhythm of plunging from turn to turn, comes from its delicious steering quality. No other car offers such crisp, responsive, lively steering feel, and the eagerness with which the F40 darts into corners is amazing. The way the wheel dances gently under your fingers, telegraphing every ridge, subtlety of surface quality and change of camber, calls to mind a Porsche 911's sublime steering, except that the F40 is better still. Wriggling like a water diviner's hazel twig, the wheel needs to be held

Below: Once you have adapted to the weight of the controls, the F40 is surprisingly easy to drive at gentle speeds. Its unassisted steering is effortless even at walking pace, clutch action sweet and engine incredibly tractable – only the brakes make the car hard work.

With fine-tuned acceleration sense, however, you find that the F40 becomes a very usable perform-ance car, not a fearsome beast which throws down a constant challenge to your driving ability.

With time you come to judge just how much of the performance can be used in any situation. Along uneven or narrow roads it is impossible to use much of the throttle because bumps transform an F40 at full-bore into a vicious, snaking beast; a more compliant 328GTB would make quicker progress in such conditions. Yet when the road becomes smoother and broader, when a clear ribbon of tarmac opens out ahead, the F40 moves into its natural habitat; an environment of gener-ous space in which all the power can be used. In normal road driving you have only fleeting mo-ments to exercise the F40 to anywhere near its true potential, but the flash of exhilaration, the joy of experiencing such outrageous performance, is quite sublime when these instants present them-selves.

always high because of the lack of servo assist-ance, but this is no handicap to progressive braking once you have learned just how hard you have to stamp. Indeed, the pedal's resistance allows it to act as a solid toe-board when you heel the throttle for a downward gearchange while braking. Despite trying some pretty serious slow-ing down, I am certain I came nowhere near to locking any wheels, so the lack of anti-lock braking – for which the F40 has been criticised – seems an academic point.

As the day wore on, my confidence in the F40 grew, my judgement improving of the driving finesse needed to obtain the best from it. So prodigious is the performance that acceleration sense has to be honed to a new pitch for your mind to keep pace with the car. If you let your concen-tration lapse for a moment while pressing on, it is easy to come barrelling up to corners, or other cars ahead, far more quickly than you think possible, leaving your braking later than is wise.

Below: Practicality played little part in the F40's design rationale, so it is not surprising to find that rearward visibility from the driver's seat can be a problem. Door mirrors give a reasonable view, but translucent plexiglass limits the interior mirror's value.

BRAKING THE BEAST
Sweet and sharp
For all the muscle needed to operate them, the brakes become better the more you use them. Having felt a little sluggish at first, they sharpen up as the giant discs, perforated sandwiches of cast iron with aluminium filling, become warmer with use. The more you attempt to punish the brakes with determined pushing, the more in-stantly and vigorously they bite. Pedal pressure is

delicately so that you can direct the car without damping its tendency to self-correct. Only with really vicious acceleration, which causes the car to squirm from side to side over bumps, is a firmer grip required.

Above: Stretching the F40's legs over the downlands of southern England. Only with . wide open spaces and a good road surface can you begin to explore the car's razor-sharp steering, balanced handling, extraordinary grip and explosive performance. So incredible is the acceleration that on uneven roads the back wheels bite and slip as the tyres struggle to put down the power.

TOTALLY IMPRACTICAL?
A question of priority

Fabulously exciting though the F40 is, no one could pretend that it is a practical car. It is engineered for unashamed speed, and to hell with convenience. During my day with it, the little irritations of living with an uncompromised sports racing car kept popping up. But for the cool blast of conditioned air through three central vents, the worst of all would be the heat which builds up in the cabin on a sunny day. Oddly enough, the top of the fascia contains two further vents to direct air to the windscreen, but I never found any means of emitting fresh air through them. The sliding side windows are maddeningly cantankerous, requiring a two-handed operation to prise them open. I began to think that it would be worth sacrificing a little lightness to have conventional wind-up glass windows, and apparently so many F40 customers have expressed the same view that this arrangement is now an option.

The lack of visibility and ear-pummelling noise are flaws which you accept as an inevitable flipside of a wind-cheating shape and pared down construction; but it can become tiresome to have to open your door and lean out to see behind when reversing the car. And as a high-speed conveyance for two people and their luggage the F40 has serious shortcomings. Those spacious door cavities are the only place to store oddments inside the car, for a battery of fuses lives where you might normally find a glovebox. There is a circular well for three pieces of Mauro Schedoni's elegant F40 luggage under the nose, but you would need your companion to help you lift this huge section of flexing bodywork.

But such carping is mean-minded as far as the F40 is concerned. Ferrari's engineers were not concerned about where you put your toothbrush or how you open the windows to pay a car park attendant. They set out to make the most extraordinary sports car in the world, and in that aim they have unquestionably succeeded. Only their opposite numbers at Stuttgart would disagree.

F40 AND THE 959
Simplicity versus complexity

The rivalry between the F40 and the Porsche 959 is much talked about. The two fastest cars in the world can achieve similar levels of performance, the lightweight F40 with 478bhp having a slight edge over the heavier 959 with 450bhp. The F40 manages 201mph (324kph) against the 959's 197mph (317kph); 0–200kph (125mph) takes 12.0sec in the F40 compared with 13.3sec in the 959. In terms of what they do the two cars are very similar, but they are poles apart in the way they do it. Thanks to the privilege of having been able to drive one of the handful of British-bound 959s 600 miles from Stuttgart to its home at the Patrick Collection in Birmingham, I have powerful memories of its character, and as I headed back towards London, the orange glow from the setting sun shimmering behind, I contemplated the question of F40 versus 959.

The only similarities I can think of are the statistical ones. In every other respect the two cars are quite astoundingly different. The F40 is a brutally raw car, immensely challenging to a driver and wildly intoxicating. The 959, for all its performance, is refined and simple to control, almost antiseptic in comparison. It is a great joy to drive, but does not demand your finest craftsmanship behind the wheel; in fact its technical package of thinking four-wheel drive, powered steering and braking, self-levelling suspension and anti-lock brakes looks after most of the donkey work for you. Much of the F40's larger-than-life character comes from its noisy, rough-riding, bellowing, extrovert presence. Sitting in the 959's lush cockpit, cocooned from the outside world by efficient sound insulation and supple suspension, is a more muted, relaxing experience.

For the man with unlimited money, having the two cars side by side in his garage would take care of all motoring needs. He would use and enjoy the 959 most of the time for supremely capable transport in all weathers, saving the F40 for a fix of really entertaining driving at weekends. I shall never own either, but should a cool million fall in my lap I know which I would choose. An F40, thank you.

INDEX

PICTURE CREDITS
The publishers wish to thank
the following
photographers and
organisations who have
supplied pictures for this
book:

Tim Andrew: 23 (below), 28
(below), 37, 40, 41, 42, 43,
44, 45, 46 (left), 54 (chapter),
56/57, 59, 62, 63.

Ferrari: 12 (below), 13, 14,
15, 16, 22, 23 (above, left
and centre)

Industrie Pininfarina SpA:
1, 11, 12 (chapter), 18, 19,
22 (above), 26, 27, 39, 64

International Press Agency
©/Jad Sherif: 47

L.A.T. Photographic Ltd: 7

Motor Trend ©: 38/39
(cutaway)

Performance Car: 4
(below), 5 (below)

All other photographs,
including endpapers and front
and back covers, were taken
by **Jim Forrest.**

Additional thanks go to
Maranello
Concessionaires Ltd of
Egham, Surrey, England,
and particularly to the
Managing Director, Roger
Maingot, for providing the
author with an F40 for the
day; to Keith and Matthew
Hopkins of KBH
Communications for their
continued support; to Allan
Mapp, also of Maranello, for
being such a good
companion. The editor is
especially grateful to Daniela
Cappa, formerly of
Pininfarina, for her
outstandng support, advice,
generosity and unfailing
good humour throughout the
preparation of this and other
books.